The Data Catalyst³ (Cubed)

Accelerating
Data Governance
with Change Management
and Data Fluency

Robert S. Seiner

Technics Publications
SEDONA, ARIZONA

I0065282

⊂⨕⊃ TECHNICS PUBLICATIONS

115 Linda Vista, Sedona, AZ 86336 USA
https://www.TechnicsPub.com

Edited by Steve Hoberman
Cover design by Lorena Molinari

All rights reserved. No part of this book may be reproduced or transmitted in any form or by any means, electronic or mechanical, including photocopying, recording, or by any information storage and retrieval system, without written permission from the publisher, except for brief quotations in a review.

The authors and publisher have taken care in the preparation of this book, but make no expressed or implied warranty of any kind and assume no responsibility for errors or omissions. No liability is assumed for incidental or consequential damages in connection with or arising out of the use of the information or programs contained herein.

All trade and product names are trademarks, registered trademarks, or service marks of their respective companies and are the property of their respective holders and should be treated as such.

Without in any way limiting the author's exclusive rights under copyright, any use of this publication to "train" generative artificial intelligence (AI) technologies to generate text is expressly prohibited. The author reserves all rights to license uses of this work for generative AI training and the development of machine learning language models.

Abstract images appearing at the beginning of most chapters were generated by ChatGPT5.

First Printing 2025
Copyright © 2025 by Robert S. Seiner

ISBN, print ed.   9798898160432
ISBN, Kindle ed.   9798898160449
ISBN, PDF ed.   9798898160456

The Catalyst Elements

How We Got Here

The story of the Data Catalyst[3] is really the story of how we, as organizations and as professionals, reached this moment in time. It's a moment defined by both promise and pressure—where AI headlines dominate boardrooms, where "data-driven" has become a universal aspiration, and where trust in information feels harder to hold onto than ever. For me, it's also a personal story—one rooted in decades of watching organizations struggle with data, stumble over governance, and ultimately discover a better, less disruptive way forward. That approach became known as Non-Invasive Data Governance (NIDG).

I didn't set out to invent a new approach to governance. I began, like many of us, inside a corporation, facing the day-to-day realities of inconsistent data, duplicated effort, and leadership teams demanding insights that the organization wasn't ready to deliver. I learned early that the traditional approaches to governance—assigning new roles, drafting thick binders of policies, and expecting culture to shift overnight—rarely worked. They created resistance instead of progress. What I saw, over and over, was that people were already governing data every day through their definitions, their decisions, and their usage. The key wasn't to add governance on top of their work. The key was to formalize and support what was already there.

That realization became the seed for what I eventually called the Non-Invasive Data Governance approach. It was governance without shackles, without disruption, and without resistance. It was practical, human, and rooted in formalized accountability instead of authority. I piloted the ideas in my corporate roles and with clients, proving again and again that organizations could make governance real without tearing themselves apart. What began as survival tactics in the corporate trenches evolved into an incredible approach—one that grew sharper, richer, and more powerful with every engagement.

The time came to share these lessons more broadly, and so my first book, *Non-Invasive Data Governance: The Path of Least Resistance and Greatest Success*, was born. It wasn't a book filled with academic theories or vendor pitches. It was a practitioner's book—one that spoke to the pain people felt and offered them a path of least resistance. That book struck a chord. It allowed people to view governance not as punishment, but as an opportunity. The acceptance was immediate and humbling.

But governance doesn't stand still. As organizations experimented with NIDG, they wanted to know what came next. That drove me to write *Non-Invasive Data Governance Strikes Again: Gaining Experience and Perspective*. Book two was about depth—in how to sustain governance once the spark had caught, how to build stewardship without assigning it, and how to embed accountability more deeply and formally across the enterprise. It built on lessons learned in the field and pushed the practice further, offering a second wave of insights that organizations could apply right away.

By the time my third book, *Non-Invasive Data Governance Unleashed: Empowering People to Govern Data and AI*, arrived, the landscape had shifted yet again. AI was no longer a distant promise. It was at the front door of every organization, demanding attention. Suddenly, governance wasn't just about compliance or efficiency. It was about trusting AI outputs, addressing bias in machine learning, and managing risk on a scale we hadn't faced before. The third book extended NIDG into the AI era, showing how the same principles that worked for traditional data could be applied to the challenges of intelligent systems.

The reception to these books exceeded my expectations. They weren't just embraced in the United States. The first book was translated into multiple languages (with the second book picking up some of that momentum), adopted by organizations across Europe, Africa, Asia, and beyond. The universality of the NIDG message—that governance could be practical, humane, and non-disruptive—resonated across cultures and industries. Partnerships with firms in Germany, South Africa, Canada, Dubai, and elsewhere became proof points that NIDG wasn't just my idea. It was becoming a global movement. Organizations of every size and sector were taking it seriously, applying it to their contexts, and proving that it worked.

As governance matured around the world, it became clear that data alone was not the only variable. If governance was to stick, it needed the disciplines of change management and data fluency (more commonly referred to as literacy) alongside it. Change management ensures adoption, helping people navigate the disruption that comes with new processes. Data fluency ensures participation, giving people the confidence and competence to use governed data effectively. Together with NIDG, these three forces created a multiplier effect—governance × change × fluency. That's how the concept of Data Catalyst[3] was born.

The word "catalyst" matters here. Too often, governance is sold as control or compliance, leaving executives skeptical, managers resentful, and practitioners disengaged. But when reframed as a catalyst, governance takes on a new energy—it becomes the spark that accelerates AI adoption, innovation, and trust. Governance, change management, and literacy don't slow organizations down. They speed them up. They multiply value instead of draining it. That is the narrative reset this book is designed to deliver.

In the world we now live in,
governed data isn't just important.
It's non-negotiable.

And so here we are with *Data Catalyst³ (Cubed)*. A book not just about governance, but about acceleration. Not just about process, but about culture. Not just about compliance, but about competitive advantage in a world defined by AI. My goal is simple but urgent—to shift the narrative once and for all. To show executives that governance is not optional, to show managers that it can reduce friction, and to show practitioners that they are already part of the solution. Most importantly, I want you to feel compelled to share these ideas with your leadership.

Overture

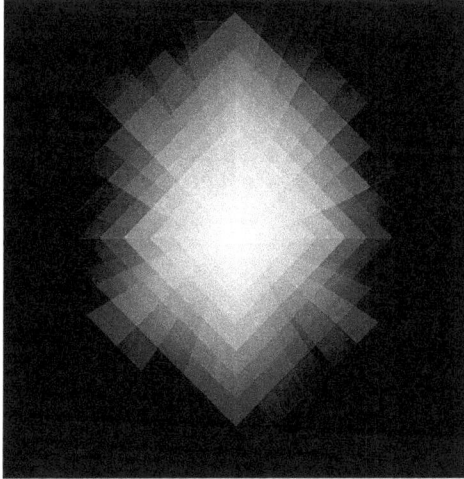

Grabbing Your Attention

Let's be honest—the words *data governance* don't usually get people sliding to the edge of their seats. In fact, if you say them in a crowded meeting, you can often hear the collective sigh ripple across the room. Governance has a reputation problem. For many, it represents bureaucracy, extra work, and more hoops to jump through before they can do their "real" jobs. And yet, at the same time, every executive boardroom is filled with conversations about AI, digital transformation, data-driven decision-making, and innovation. It's a strange paradox—organizations want all the benefits of modern data and technology, but they hesitate when it comes to the very thing that makes it possible—governing the data.

The irony is that governance isn't the enemy of speed or creativity. It's the missing ingredient that allows organizations to move faster without falling apart. Imagine building a skyscraper without a blueprint or racing a car without brakes. You might feel the thrill of progress—but only until you realize you've put everyone and everything at risk. The same applies to data. Without governance, people can't trust what they're using, can't share it effectively, and can't rely on it to power decisions. When governance is done right, especially through a Non-Invasive approach, it doesn't slow you down. It accelerates everything else.

What if governance wasn't about adding friction,
but about removing it?

What if the disciplines we often view as chores—governance, change management, and data literacy—were actually the catalysts for unlocking the promises of AI, analytics, and better decision-making? That's the spark we're going to ignite together.

Non-Invasive Data Governance in Context

The truth is that many organizations have already tried the "traditional" route to data governance—and most have the scars to prove it. They've launched big initiatives with shiny tools and lofty goals, only to see them collapse under their own weight. Some tried to assign "data stewards" out of thin air, hoping new titles would solve old problems. Others wrote lengthy policies that no one ever read, let alone followed. The results? Frustration, fatigue, and the kind of eye-rolling that ensures governance doesn't stand a chance the next time it's brought up.

Non-Invasive Data Governance (NIDG) emerged from this reality. I developed it because I saw how organizations were tripping over themselves, trying to force governance on people instead of working with how people already interact with data. NIDG takes a different route. It recognizes that people are *already* governing data—defining it, producing it, using it—every single day. The job isn't to create governance from scratch, but to make it formal, consistent, and transparent in ways that strengthen trust rather than disrupt business. It's about leveraging existing roles, responsibilities, and processes to build a culture of accountability without the resistance that comes from adding "extra" tasks.

In this book, NIDG becomes the foundation upon which the other two catalysts—change management and data fluency—stand. Governance alone, even when done non-invasively, still struggles to gain momentum if people resist change or don't understand data. But when governance is combined with the disciplines of change and fluency, suddenly the lights come on. Data governance becomes not just a compliance function, but a living, breathing accelerator that delivers value across the entire organization—from the C-suite to the front line.

A Quick Word for Non-Invasive Detractors

There will always be critics who believe that data governance must be invasive to be effective. They equate authority with disruption, assuming that unless governance is imposed with new titles, rigid structures, and top-down mandates, it won't withstand audits or deliver results. These skeptics hear the phrase *Non-Invasive Data Governance* and immediately jump to the conclusion that "non-invasive" means soft, optional, or ineffective. But that is a fundamental misunderstanding. Non-invasive does not remove the teeth from governance—it simply delivers those teeth in a way that people can live with.

> *The result of any governance program must be*
> *to execute and enforce authority over data.*

That is the non-negotiable "what" of governance. Policies must be followed, standards must be applied, and accountabilities must be enforced. Without that, there is no governance. Where the difference lies is in the *how*. Traditional governance attempts to overlay new processes, roles, and layers of bureaucracy on top of existing operations. Non-Invasive Data Governance takes a different route: it embeds accountability into the work people already do, clarifies and formalizes their existing responsibilities, and makes those responsibilities visible and auditable without overwhelming the culture.

Skeptics often argue that anything less than invasive governance will be ignored. Yet the opposite is often true. Invasive governance frequently creates resistance, slows adoption, and generates endless "shadow practices" as people work around rules they perceive as impractical. By contrast, a non-invasive approach reduces resistance by respecting the way people already interact with data. It makes governance feel natural and necessary, rather than bolted on and burdensome. The authority remains, but it is enforced through integration rather than interruption.

Non-invasive is not about being passive;
it's about being effective.

It is not governance without enforcement—it is governance without the cultural antibodies that kill adoption. If the purpose of governance is to make data reliable, trusted, and fit for use in decision-making, then the best way to achieve that is to deliver governance in a manner the organization will embrace, not reject. Non-Invasive Data Governance ensures that the outcome—authority over data—is never compromised. However, the path to achieve it is one that people can support, sustain, and scale. That's not a weakness. That's wisdom.

Set the Stage: Why One Discipline Is Not Enough

On its own, governance can provide accountability and structure. On its own, change management can facilitate smooth transitions and maintain alignment when strategies shift. On its own, data fluency can give employees more confidence in working with data. But when they remain isolated, each discipline hits a ceiling. Governance without change management becomes a set of rules people quietly ignore. Change management without governance becomes theater—plenty of workshops and communication, but no solid foundation to anchor it. Data fluency without governance or change is like teaching people to drive on roads that haven't been paved—they learn skills, but they can't apply them consistently or safely.

That's why I call this concept **catalyst cubed**—governance × change × fluency. The power isn't in each discipline individually, but in how they multiply each other's impact. Together, they create acceleration. Governance provides the trust and structure. Change management ensures adoption and sustainability. Literacy makes data accessible and usable to everyone. When they work in unison, the organization doesn't just move forward—it moves forward with confidence, speed, and shared understanding.

Why I Use the Term Data Fluency Instead of Data Literacy

By talking about fluency rather than literacy, we acknowledge that data is no longer a static text to be read. It's a dynamic language to be spoken and understood. This subtle but important shift in language reflects the way the data landscape has evolved, and why the term fluency feels more in tune with the demands of our digital and AI-driven age. As organizations strive to integrate governance, change management, and human understanding to unlock the true value of data, fluency feels like the concept that meets the moment: a signal that we're ready not just to read data but to speak its language with confidence.

For the balance of this book, I will proceed with the understanding that data fluency is "the ability of people across an organization to confidently understand, communicate, and apply data in context to make informed decisions and drive measurable outcomes." You will find the term data literacy sprinkled throughout the book as appropriate as well.

This book isn't just about convincing you of that synergy. It's about showing you how to bring it to life. We'll walk through real-world stories of organizations that have stumbled and succeeded, we'll dismantle myths that hold governance back, and we'll provide practical playbooks you can apply at every level of your business. Whether you're an executive deciding where to invest, a manager translating strategy into practice, or a practitioner working hands-on with data, you'll find ways to connect the dots and see the "cubed" effect at work.

What's Ahead?

So, what should you expect as you turn the pages? First, expect plain talk. This is not a book filled with academic jargon or technology buzzwords that make sense only to vendors. It's written for the people who actually need to make governance, change, and literacy work—people like you, no matter your level or role. Second, expect practical steps. Theory is essential, but without application, it doesn't stick. Each section of the book includes both the "why" and the "how," providing you with playbooks and practices that you can test immediately in your organization. Most importantly, expect a shift in perspective. If you came into this book thinking governance was about control, change management was about endless meetings, and data literacy was just a series of training sessions nobody wanted to attend, I promise you'll walk away with a different view. You'll see these disciplines as multipliers of value, not drains on energy. You'll see how they can accelerate AI adoption, improve decision-making, reduce organizational drama, and, perhaps most importantly, restore trust in the data your business depends on.

That's the journey of *Data Catalyst³*. By the end, you'll not only understand how governance, change, and literacy connect, you'll be equipped to make them come alive in your own world. And when you do, you'll discover that data isn't just a burden to manage. It's a catalyst for innovation, trust, and success in a world that demands nothing less.

ONE

Igniting the Catalyst

Why We Need a Spark

Organizations have been talking about being "data-driven" for decades, but the reality often falls short of the promise. Ask an executive what keeps them up at night, and they'll point to inconsistent reports, risky AI models, or regulatory requirements that feel impossible to stay ahead of. Ask a manager, and they'll discuss silos, redundant work, and the constant firefighting required to reconcile numbers before submitting them to upper management. Ask practitioners, including analysts, engineers, and everyday business users, and you'll often hear a quiet frustration: "We don't trust the data."

That frustration is often referred to as **data fatigue**. People become worn down from chasing after numbers that don't align, systems that don't communicate, and governance programs that feel like "one more thing to do." Fatigue turns into skepticism, and skepticism kills momentum. This is why so many organizations see AI initiatives stumble, analytics projects stall, and "data transformation" turn into another buzzword that fizzles out. The missing piece isn't technology or funding. It's spark. Without a catalyst to cut through the fatigue and reignite energy, even the best-designed initiatives risk becoming shelfware.

Today's priority isn't just managing data,
it's accelerating results.

That acceleration can't come from tools alone, nor can it come from slogans about being "data-driven." It comes from aligning governance, change, and fluency in ways that energize rather than drain. Think of it like striking a match. On its own, a match won't keep you warm. But light the right tinder—in this case, governance practices people can live with, change approaches people will adopt, and fluency that feels relevant to their jobs—and you'll build a fire that lasts.

Cubed, Not Doubled

At first glance, you might wonder: why "cubed"? Why not just say "triple the effect" or "three disciplines together"?

Governance sets the framework of accountability. Change management ensures that the framework doesn't sit on a shelf but comes alive in how people work. Fluency ensures everyone understands not just the rules, but the *why* behind them—building literacy so that data is no longer intimidating, but empowering. Multiply those together and you get acceleration at every level of the organization. Executives make faster, more confident decisions. Managers see smoother adoption and fewer "workarounds." Practitioners stop reinventing the wheel and start contributing value right away.

*When you combine governance, change
management, and fluency,
you don't just add one on top of another.
They multiply each other's impact.*

Think of a relay race. If governance runs its leg but hands the baton to a poorly designed change initiative, the team stumbles. If change makes progress, but fluency hasn't prepared the runners, the baton gets dropped. However, when all three are trained, coordinated, and aligned, the baton passes seamlessly from hand to hand, and the whole team crosses the finish line together. That's why this is more than addition. It's multiplication. It's cubed.

Busting the Myths of Data Catalysts

Of course, when discussing governance, change, and literacy as accelerators, some people roll their eyes. Let's tackle those myths head-on. First, there's the myth that governance slows things down. That may be true in traditional, heavy-handed approaches. But in a Non-Invasive model, governance is about clarifying roles and expectations so people can work faster, not slower. It eliminates the endless second-guessing about "whose data is right" and provides a clear path to trusted outcomes.

Second, there's the myth that fluency, and also literacy, is just training. Ask anyone who's sat through a mandatory training session and promptly forgotten everything by lunch, and they'll tell you—training alone doesn't change behavior. Literacy is about fluency. It's about equipping people to think, question, and act with data as naturally as they communicate in their own language. When organizations invest in fluency, they stop treating data as someone else's problem and start weaving it into their own decision-making.

And finally, there's the myth that change is optional. Many executives still believe that if you roll out a tool or policy, people will "get on board."

Experience says otherwise. Resistance is a natural human response and ignoring it only ensures it festers. Effective change management isn't about forcing compliance—it's about harnessing resistance as feedback, adjusting approaches, and giving people ownership of the process. Change isn't an optional extra. It's the discipline that makes everything else stick.

Governance doesn't have to mean bureaucracy.
Fluency doesn't have to mean training binders.
Change doesn't have to mean drama.

Why the Spark Matters

Organizations today are under pressure unlike anything we've seen before. From disruption to AI, from lost trust to resistance fatigue, the climate is unpredictable and unforgiving. To ignite the catalyst, you must first understand why a spark is so crucial at this moment. These reasons give data governance practitioners the fuel they need to position governance, change management, and fluency as essential accelerators, not optional extras.

- **Constant Disruption**: Organizations no longer operate in predictable cycles. Disruption comes from every direction: supply chain crises, rapid technology shifts, geopolitical events, and sudden changes in consumer behavior. For a data governance practitioner, this unpredictability means that old, rigid governance approaches won't work. A spark is needed to help governance feel like a tool for agility, not rigidity. When governance, change management, and fluency combine, they provide a stabilizing force in chaotic times—a catalyst that helps the business pivot without losing trust in its data.

- **AI Moving Faster Than Control**: Artificial intelligence has shifted from experimentation to execution at a speed that has caught many leaders by surprise. Models are being deployed without adequate governance over the data that feeds them. The spark is needed to remind executives that AI cannot be trusted without governed data, and practitioners must act as both voices of caution and acceleration. Governance in this context doesn't slow down innovation—it ensures innovation is sustainable. Without the spark, organizations risk running faster into risk.

- **Erosion of Trust in Data**: Trust in data remains one of the greatest barriers to becoming data-driven. Executives doubt the dashboards. Managers question conflicting reports. Practitioners struggle with systems that don't align. The spark is needed because fatigue and skepticism are real. People want to trust data but have been burned too many times. By igniting the catalyst, you reframe governance as the path back to trust—not through top-down enforcement, but by embedding accountability and fluency into everyday work. Trust isn't built overnight, but without the spark, it may never be rebuilt at all.

- **Decision Velocity Outpacing Governance**: The pace of decision-making has accelerated. Leaders are pressured to make decisions faster than ever, sometimes in real-time. Yet governance hasn't always kept up with that velocity. The spark is needed to align governance practices with the modern pace of decision-making. For practitioners, this means ensuring definitions, stewardship, and literacy are built into workflows so that governance is "in the flow" of decisions, not lagging behind them. For executives, it's reassurance that faster doesn't have to mean riskier.

- **Resistance Fatigue**: Every organization has experienced "initiative fatigue"—too many projects, too many changes, too many promises that never delivered. Resistance is natural, but fatigue is dangerous because it can cause disengagement. The spark is needed to reignite energy by reframing governance not as one more initiative but as an accelerator of existing priorities. For practitioners, this means demonstrating value quickly and visibly. For executives, it means demanding proof that governance speeds things up rather than adding burden. The spark combats fatigue by showing that governance is a solution, not another problem.

Ways to Spark the Catalyst

Artifacts to Consider Building

While sparking the catalyst begins with mindset, it quickly becomes a reality when supported by practical tools and artifacts that practitioners can build and utilize. These artifacts translate ideas into action, giving governance, change management, and fluency a tangible presence in the organization. The following list—and similar lists shared throughout the book— highlight examples of artifacts, with one detailed in the Field Guide, that can potentially serve as accelerators—helping to reduce resistance, embed accountability, and spread fluency in ways that are visible, usable, and repeatable.

1. Data Catalyst³ Spark Alignment Checklist

The first tool practitioners can build is a **Data Catalyst³ Spark Alignment Checklist**—a short, repeatable list of actions that validate whether governance, change, and fluency are being ignited within a project or initiative. This checklist might include items such as: Have governance roles been clearly defined? Has resistance been acknowledged and addressed? Have literacy needs been assessed and met? Is the spark visible to executives and practitioners alike?

The value of the checklist is its simplicity. It takes a large, conceptual idea—"igniting the spark"—and turns it into a practical tool for practitioners to use in workshops, meetings, or project planning. When checked off consistently, it demonstrates progress and builds confidence that the spark isn't just theory, but something tangible and visible.

---

*See how to develop and use this artifact
in the Field Guide at the end of the book.*

---

2. Messaging & Myth-Busting Narrative

Resistance often comes from misconceptions: "governance slows us down," "change management is theater," or "data fluency is just training." Practitioners can create a **Messaging & Myth-Busting Narrative**. This structured communication plan identifies common myths about governance, change, and fluency, accompanied by clear, positive reframes that align with the Data Catalyst[3] perspective.

This deliverable becomes a powerful communication tool for executives and managers who need to carry the message upward and outward. It provides them with simple, repeatable stories that challenge old narratives and ignite new ones. When consistently shared, these reframed messages shift perception and spark curiosity rather than skepticism.

3. Spark Communication Plan

A **Spark Communication Plan** is a lightweight roadmap for how to talk about Data Catalyst[3] within an organization. It defines who needs to hear the message (executives, managers, practitioners), what they need to hear (value, efficiency, trust), and when they need to hear it (launch, quick wins, milestones). The plan ensures that communication is consistent and catalytic rather than ad hoc.

For practitioners, this plan is critical because it prevents the spark from being a one-time "kickoff" moment that fizzles out. Instead, it institutionalizes communication as part of the spark itself. Regular, targeted, and reinforcing communication creates momentum and keeps the spark alive across levels of the organization.

4. Data Catalyst³ Multiplication Model

One of the most compelling ways to illustrate the spark is through a **Data Catalyst³ Multiplication Model**—a simple diagram or outline showing how governance, change management, and fluency combine not additively, but multiplicatively. The model can highlight the value of each discipline alone and then show the exponential impact when combined.

This model helps practitioners translate a complex concept into a visual or narrative that executives and managers can grasp quickly. It demonstrates that governance on its own may stall, change management without governance may fade, and fluency and literacy without structure may confuse—but cubed together, they accelerate progress and value. This model can serve as both a teaching tool and a rallying point for igniting the spark.

Actions to Take

The idea of a catalyst only matters if it sparks movement. Data Catalyst³ isn't theory for the sake of theory—it's about multiplication, acceleration, and momentum. The moment you start combining governance, change management, and fluency, you stop adding value linearly and start multiplying it exponentially. But to feel that multiplication, you must ignite the spark.

That spark often starts with reframing. If your colleagues think governance slows things down, or literacy is just training, or change is optional, those myths must be dismantled. Igniting the catalyst means introducing new language, new stories, and new evidence that proves governance can be fast, engaging, and valuable.

Executives, managers, and practitioners alike can play this role. Executives can demand acceleration, not just compliance. Managers can test small experiments that prove governance saves time. Practitioners can call out and celebrate wins where governance has made their jobs easier. Every time you light a spark, you make it easier for the next flame to catch.

The choice is simple: keep fighting fatigue or ignite the catalyst. Once the spark is visible, momentum spreads. And when momentum spreads, the cube comes alive.

Immediate Actionable Steps

1. Identify and debunk one myth about governance, change, or fluency in your organization.

2. Share a story that reframes governance or fluency as an accelerator, not an obstacle.

3. Pilot one small change that demonstrates governance saves time or reduces friction.

4. Facilitate a short discussion with your team about how resistance can be reframed as energy.

5. Create a simple, shareable visual (even on a whiteboard) that illustrates the multiplication effect of governance × change × fluency.

Two

Data Governance as a Catalyst

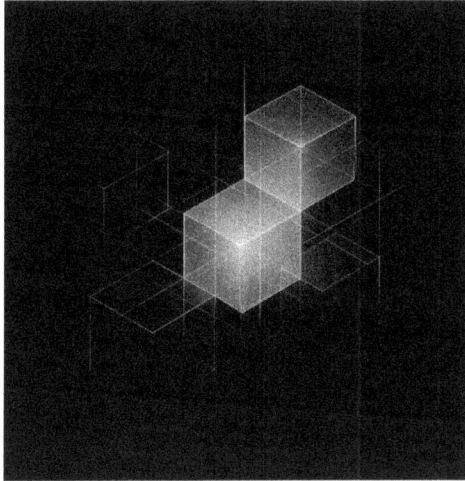

Part A: Theory

Governance Without Shackles

For years, governance has been portrayed as the corporate equivalent of handcuffs—a set of rigid rules designed to keep people from stepping out of line. That image is powerful, but it's also wrong. When governance is treated as shackles, people resist it. They find workarounds. They delay adoption. They quietly create shadow systems that undermine trust and introduce risk. And then, ironically, the very leaders who thought governance would bring order are left with even more chaos.

The Non-Invasive Data Governance approach changes that. Instead of imposing new responsibilities, it recognizes that people are already governing data in their daily work—whether they admit it or not. Executives are making strategic decisions based on dashboards. Managers are reconciling reports. Practitioners are defining, creating, and using data in ways that affect the entire business. The "invasive" mistake organizations make is trying to bolt governance on top of this reality. The smarter play is to meet people where they already are and formalize the accountability they're already demonstrating.

For executives, this means governance doesn't feel like another initiative competing for budget. It becomes the enabler that allows AI, analytics, and transformation to succeed. For managers, it means governance isn't a policing function—it's a framework that helps their teams work faster and avoid rework. For practitioners, it means governance isn't an interruption to their jobs—it's embedded in their jobs. This is governance without shackles: liberating rather than restraining.

When most people hear the words data governance, they immediately picture restrictions, bureaucracy, and more hurdles in their path. The Non-Invasive approach flips that perception by showing that governance, when delivered thoughtfully, is about clarity, acceleration, and alignment rather than shackles. Table 1 helps clarify the contrast by illustrating how governance can be either obstructive or catalytic, depending on its implementation.

Dimension	Traditional / Invasive Governance	Non-Invasive Governance (Catalyst)
Accountability	Assigned, often resisted	Recognized, role-based, accepted
Adoption	Mandated, compliance-driven	Embedded, natural, self-sustaining
Perception	Extra burden, slows projects	Enabler, accelerates decisions
Integration	Bolt-on, disruptive	Built-in, non-disruptive
Value	Hard to demonstrate, abstract	Visible through metrics and wins

Table 1: Invasive Versus Non-Invasive Governance Implementation Comparison

Accountability Over Authority

The difference between accountability and authority might seem subtle, but it's the heart of why so many governance programs fail. Authority relies on enforcement: someone at the top declares, "this is how it will be," and expects compliance to follow. Accountability, by contrast, is about owning your role in defining, producing, and using data responsibly. It's less about enforcing rules and more about reinforcing responsibilities that already exist.

Executives don't need to be told they're accountable for the decisions they make with data, but they do need visibility into whether the data behind those decisions can be trusted. Managers don't need to be handed a list of new rules, but they do need clarity on who is responsible when metrics don't add up. Practitioners don't need to be micromanaged, but they do need confidence that the definitions and standards they rely on are consistent across the organization.

> *When accountability becomes the focus, people stop feeling like governance is being "done to them."*

Authority creates friction. Accountability creates alignment. In a world where speed matters, alignment wins every time.

Trust as the True Product of Governance

Organizations often measure governance by the number of policies written, the number of stewards assigned, or the number of issues logged. These metrics have their place, but they overlook the broader context. The real output of governance isn't documents or dashboards. It's trust. Executives need to trust that the AI models they invest in won't collapse under the weight of bad data. Managers need to trust that when their teams deliver numbers, those numbers won't be contradicted two slides later. Practitioners need to trust that when they raise their hand with a data quality concern, someone will listen and act. Without trust, governance devolves into bureaucracy. With trust, governance becomes a catalyst for innovation and speed.

Trust also travels fast. When one part of the organization sees that governance is working—that definitions are clear, that issues are resolved, that quality is improving—it creates momentum that spreads naturally. This is why Non-Invasive Governance focuses not on authority, but on cultivating trust. Ultimately, trust is what fuels adoption, sustains change, and opens the door for innovation to thrive.

Part B: Practice and Playbook

Embedding Governance into Daily Work

The fastest way to kill a governance initiative is to make it feel like an extra layer of work. People are already busy enough, and "more tasks" will never be a selling point. The key is embedding governance directly into the processes people already follow. This might involve linking data definitions to project templates, so teams don't have to search for them. It may include integrating stewardship roles into existing workflows rather than creating new meetings. It may involve utilizing the systems people already rely on, such as collaboration platforms, catalogs, and reporting tools, to surface governance in context. For executives, embedding governance involves ensuring that governance processes are integrated into strategic decision-making cycles rather than being added as an afterthought. For managers, it means governance checkpoints are integrated into the project lifecycle, not dropped in at the end. For practitioners, it means governance is present at the point of use—the moment they define, produce, or consume data—so it feels natural rather than forced.

> *When governance is embedded,*
> *it stops feeling like a compliance activity*
> *and begins to feel like muscle memory.*

Building Muscles Through Stewardship

Think of governance as a workout program for your organization. You don't get stronger overnight—you build muscles through consistent, repeated actions. Stewardship is how those muscles develop. But stewardship doesn't mean handing out new job titles or recruiting a brand-new class of "data stewards." In the Non-Invasive approach, stewardship is about recognizing and supporting the people who already have relationships with the data. These people know how it's defined, how it's used, and where it breaks down.

Executives can model stewardship by sponsoring initiatives and showing they take accountability seriously. Managers can model stewardship by championing consistency in their areas and encouraging their teams to bring issues to light early. Practitioners can model stewardship by documenting and sharing what they already know about data, instead of keeping that knowledge tribal and hidden.

The payoff comes when stewardship becomes normalized. Instead of a few "appointed" stewards doing all the heavy lifting, the entire organization contributes. That's when the governance muscles get strong enough to carry the weight of AI, analytics, and transformation initiatives without collapsing.

Measuring the Acceleration

If you want executives to invest in governance, managers to prioritize it, and practitioners to adopt it, you need evidence that it's effective. The trick is to measure governance not by how much it slows things down, but by how much it speeds things up. Executives want to see risk reduced and time-to-insight shortened. Show them that projects are hitting targets faster because governance has eliminated endless debates over whose numbers are "right." Managers want to see productivity gains. Show them that fewer hours are wasted reconciling reports or fixing avoidable mistakes. Practitioners want to see their work valued. Show them that when they raise an issue, it gets resolved quickly and visibly, saving them time in the long run.

The most powerful governance metrics aren't the ones that count documents or roles. They're the ones that demonstrate acceleration. Projects are delivered faster. Insights are trusted more widely. AI models perform more reliably. When you measure those outcomes, governance shifts from a "cost center" to a "catalyst." And once people see that, the buy-in takes care of itself.

Why Governance Accelerates

Data governance practitioners often find themselves explaining why governance is important in the first place. This section provides the grounding arguments: governance accelerates business value because it builds accountability, trust, efficiency, and proof. These are not abstract benefits—they are measurable and visible outcomes when governance is practiced in a Non-Invasive way.

- **Accountability Builds Alignment**: Without accountability, data remains fragmented. Different teams make different decisions, and executives get frustrated by inconsistent results. Accountability doesn't mean authority—it means clarity about who is responsible. For practitioners, accountability removes confusion about ownership. For managers, it eliminates duplication. For executives, it aligns the enterprise so decisions flow faster and more consistently.
- **Trust Unlocks Adoption**: No one adopts what they don't trust. If executives doubt reports, they delay action. If managers question metrics, they delay delivery. If practitioners mistrust their tools, they find workarounds. Trust is the accelerant that makes governance valuable. Building trust through transparency and stewardship ensures people want to use governed data because they know it won't embarrass them later.
- **Embedded Practices Save Time**: Governance bolted on at the end feels like bureaucracy. Governance embedded into daily work feels like muscle memory. Practitioners stop seeing governance as "extra work" when it's woven into their workflows. Managers appreciate fewer escalations. Executives

appreciate smoother projects. Embedded practices don't add steps; they remove rework, which is why governance accelerates instead of obstructs.

- **Stewardship Spreads Knowledge**: Knowledge gaps create bottlenecks. When only a handful of people understand data definitions or rules, projects stall waiting for answers. Stewardship spreads that knowledge naturally, so accountability isn't concentrated but distributed. Practitioners share their knowledge, managers champion clarity, and executives see expertise expanding across the business. Spreading stewardship accelerates access to answers.

- **Metrics Demonstrate Value**: Executives fund what they can measure. Managers prioritize what they can track. Practitioners commit to what they see working. Governance accelerates when metrics prove its worth—fewer errors, faster projects, smoother audits. These metrics shift governance from "theory" to "evidence," ensuring support at every level.

Theory only takes us so far; the true test of governance is how it shows up in practice. Practitioners and leaders alike want to see how principles of Non-Invasive Data Governance translate into day-to-day work. Table 2 provides a simplified view of where governance can be embedded directly into existing processes, demonstrating that governance in action doesn't slow down work—it makes it smoother, clearer, and more consistent.

Business Process	Without Governance	With NIDG Embedded
Project Planning	Unclear data ownership, scope creep	Defined roles, clear data deliverables
Decision-Making	Conflicting metrics, mistrust	Single source of truth, trusted dashboards
Operations	Reactive problem-solving	Proactive accountability, fewer escalations
Compliance/Audit	Scramble for reports, gaps	Evidence ready, reduced risk
AI/Analytics	Model failure, bias exposure	Trusted inputs, scalable results

Table 2: Business Processes Comparison
Without Versus With Embedded Governance

Ways to Apply Governance as a Catalyst

Artifacts to Consider Building

Applying governance as a catalyst means moving beyond theory and embedding it directly into the way work gets done. To make this shift practical, practitioners can create simple but powerful artifacts that clarify accountability, reinforce trust, and show value quickly. These artifacts provide structure without adding unnecessary burden, making governance feel like an enabler rather than an obstacle. The following list highlights examples of artifacts that potentially can bring governance to life in visible and actionable ways.

1. Accountability Alignment Matrix

One of the most useful tools a practitioner can create is an **Accountability Alignment Matrix**. This simple template maps data domains or processes against the roles already accountable for them. Rather than assigning new responsibilities, the matrix highlights where accountability already exists and makes it explicit. By doing so, it clarifies confusion, reduces duplication, and makes it easier for executives and managers to determine where responsibility lies.

The value of this deliverable lies in reinforcing the Non-Invasive Data Governance principle: governance doesn't require new titles; it requires clarity around existing ones. For practitioners, the matrix becomes a repeatable artifact they can use to guide conversations with leaders and teams, demonstrating that governance accelerates alignment rather than creating new bureaucracy.

*See how to develop and use this artifact
in the Field Guide at the end of the book.*

2. Trust-Building Playbook

Executives, managers, and practitioners often struggle with the same issue: they lack trust in the data. A **Trust-Building Playbook** provides a structured set of practices to identify where trust is eroded (e.g., conflicting reports, inconsistent definitions, poor-quality inputs) and outlines steps to restore it. This playbook may include quick-win actions, such as aligning on a single definition of a critical term, documenting data lineage, or resolving a recurring quality issue transparently.

By producing and socializing this playbook, practitioners can demonstrate that trust isn't rebuilt through speeches—it's rebuilt through consistent actions. The playbook becomes a living document that can be updated over time, providing leaders with a clear narrative: governance isn't slowing us down; it's the accelerator for rebuilding credibility and confidence in decision-making.

3. Embedded Governance Workflow Guide

One of the most powerful ways to accelerate governance is to make it invisible. Practitioners can develop an **Embedded Governance Workflow Guide**—a practical outline of how governance can be integrated directly into existing business processes, project lifecycles, or system workflows. Instead of creating new steps, the guide shows how governance checkpoints (definitions, stewardship, validation) can be layered into what people already do.

The guide is valuable because it transforms governance from "something extra" into "the way we work." Managers experience fewer escalations, practitioners encounter fewer conflicts, and executives achieve smoother outcomes. For practitioners, the guide becomes a repeatable tool they can adapt to multiple teams, proving that embedding governance saves time rather than consumes it.

4. Stewardship Role Narrative

Too often, stewardship is misunderstood as a title rather than a responsibility. A **Stewardship Role Narrative** provides a simple communication artifact that explains what stewardship means in practice, how it already exists within roles, and why it accelerates access to answers and spreads knowledge. The narrative can be delivered as a short explainer document, a set of talking points, or even a one-page story showing stewardship in action.

The importance of this narrative is its ability to reframe stewardship as empowering rather than burdensome. Practitioners can use it to engage colleagues who may not realize they are already acting as stewards. Executives and managers can use it to reinforce the value of stewardship without threatening people with new titles or responsibilities. This narrative makes stewardship practical, relatable, and non-invasive.

5. Governance Metrics Dashboard Outline

Executives will only sustain support for governance if they can see evidence of its value. A **Governance Metrics Dashboard Outline** provides practitioners with a structured starting point for tracking the right indicators, including reduced rework, faster project delivery, smoother audits, increased trust scores, and the adoption of governed data assets. The outline doesn't need to be a fully built tool—it can simply be a model of what to measure and why.

This deliverable is powerful because it ties governance to outcomes that matter to leadership. When executives see metrics, they shift from questioning "Why do we need governance?" to asking "How do we get more of this?" Practitioners who develop a metrics outline position governance as measurable acceleration, not abstract compliance. It becomes the proof point that governance is worth investing in.

Actions to Take

Governance without shackles, built on accountability and trust, is more than a framework—it's a way of working. You've seen how Non-Invasive Data Governance meets people where they are, embedding stewardship into existing roles and ensuring trust is the true product. But knowledge without action is wasted. This is where you put theory into practice.

Don't think of governance as a project with a start and finish. Think of it as muscle-building—small, consistent actions that get stronger over time. Every time you clarify a definition, embed stewardship in daily workflows, or resolve an issue transparently, you strengthen the governance muscle. The stronger it gets, the faster the organization moves.

Trust is earned, not declared. If you want executives to invest, managers to support, and practitioners to participate, you need proof that governance accelerates results. Show how projects run faster, audits run smoother, and reports gain confidence when governance is embedded. Those stories are your fuel.

Embed it, measure it, celebrate it—
and you'll transform governance from
an obligation into a competitive advantage.

Immediate Actionable Steps

1. Identify one process where governance can be embedded into existing workflows.

2. Recognize and support at least one person already acting as a data steward in practice.

3. Define one metric that demonstrates governance accelerates (e.g., reduced rework, faster reports).

4. Share one governance success story with leadership that highlights trust, not compliance.

5. Establish a repeatable method to log and resolve data issues transparently.

THREE

Change Management as a Catalyst

Part A: Theory

Change Without the Drama

The mere mention of "change management" can spark groans almost as loud as "data governance." People pictured endless slide decks, consultants camped out in conference rooms and forced cheerleading for initiatives that quietly fizzled a few months later. It doesn't help that many change programs in the past were rolled out as events instead of ongoing processes, promising transformation but delivering disruption.

---

*Drama builds when people feel things are being done **to** them instead of **with** them.*

That drama can derail even the best technical strategies before they gain traction.

But real change management, especially when applied to data and governance, is not about hype or theatrics. It's about carefully reducing uncertainty, creating clarity, and pacing progress in ways that people can absorb. Effective change recognizes that every shift—from a new AI tool to a new way of defining metrics—challenges habits that may have been built over years. Drama-free change is about acknowledging this reality and designing pathways that respect people's capacity to adapt without overwhelming them.

Executives should see change management not as an optional line item but as insurance for their investments. The millions spent on platforms, analytics, and AI are wasted if people resist adoption or revert to old ways of working. Managers should see change as a leadership skill, not a project burden—guiding their teams through uncertainty with consistency and patience. Practitioners should view change as an opportunity to shape the future of their own work, rather than something imposed by outsiders.

Change often gets a bad reputation because it's associated with resistance, confusion, and drama. But change doesn't have to feel like upheaval—when handled deliberately, it can be a smooth process that guides people rather than overwhelms them. The Non-Invasive approach to change management treats resistance as information, adoption as a psychological process, and progress as a series of achievable wins. Table 3 contrasts how traditional approaches often generate drama versus how Catalyst³ reframes change to accelerate adoption.

Dimension	Traditional Change (with Drama)	Catalyst[3] Change (Without Drama)
Resistance	Viewed as a failure to comply	Treated as insight into priorities
Adoption	Mandated, compliance-driven	Rooted in ownership and fairness
Momentum	Big-bang launches, fragile	Built through small wins, sustainable
Leadership	One sponsor, top-down voice	Distributed champions at all levels
Communication	Policy-heavy, impersonal	Story-driven, human-centered

Table 3: With Drama Versus Without Drama
Change Management Implementation Comparison

When change management shifts its focus from drama to enabling people, it becomes the silent strength of governance programs. It ensures that new practices don't flame out as fleeting initiatives but instead become natural parts of how the organization functions. That quiet strength is why change management is governance's secret ally—a partner that doesn't steal the spotlight but makes sure the show can go on.

Resistance is Data Energy

Resistance to change is often painted as stubbornness, laziness, or defiance. In truth, resistance is energy—people who care enough to push back, to question, and to voice their concerns. Indifference is the real enemy—because when people no longer care, they stop engaging altogether. Resistance, on the other hand, indicates where the organization experiences tension, confusion, or risk. And tension is valuable. It signals where leaders need to focus.

Executives often misinterpret resistance as failure, assuming that if people aren't on board immediately, the initiative must be flawed. Instead, executives should view resistance as feedback loops that highlight what matters most to their teams. If managers hear objections, that's not a sign to clamp down—it's a sign to listen more carefully and clarify benefits. For practitioners, resistance can be a protective instinct, guarding against workload overload or poorly thought-out processes. Validating these instincts creates credibility, even before resolution begins.

Channeling resistance requires empathy and structure—leaders who invite feedback and adjust accordingly turn skeptics into allies. Managers who acknowledge the disruption while showing the eventual upside win trust faster than those who dismiss concerns—practitioners who feel heard become champions, rather than critics. By framing resistance as energy, organizations can utilize it as fuel to enhance adoption, rather than as a barrier to be eliminated.

The difference between momentum and gridlock is often in how resistance is handled. Treated as opposition, it breeds conflict. Treated as energy, it propels governance forward, making adoption stronger and stickier. In the world of data governance, where clarity and trust are already hard-won, harnessing resistance effectively can mean the difference between another failed rollout and a sustainable cultural shift.

The Psychology of Data Adoption

Adoption isn't just about rules and incentives—it's about psychology. People don't embrace new ways of working because they were told to. They embrace them because the change aligns with their sense of identity, competence, and control. If governance or literacy initiatives make people feel less competent, less autonomous, or less valued, resistance spikes. If they make people feel more capable, more connected, and more trusted, adoption becomes a natural choice.

Executives need to understand that adoption at scale isn't about issuing a mandate. It's about storytelling and example-setting. When leaders use governed dashboards in their own decision-making and highlight the value they see, they send signals that resonate more deeply than any memo. Managers need to be consistent role models, reinforcing desired behaviors through small wins and recognition, rather than just enforcing processes. Practitioners, in turn, adopt most readily when they feel ownership—when they see how data adoption makes their own jobs easier, safer, and more respected. The psychology of adoption also relies on the perception of fairness. If governance feels like it's applied selectively—if some teams are held to higher standards while others are given a free pass—adoption collapses. People must recognize that the changes are universal, that no one is exempt from the principles being promoted.

Fairness, transparency, and visible accountability all contribute to a sense that adoption is not just possible but expected.

When adoption becomes part of the organization's identity, governance doesn't feel like a burden. It feels like culture. And once it's a cultural issue, the psychological resistance fades. People don't just comply because they have to. They embrace governance because it fits how they already think about their work and their organization's mission.

Part B: Practice and Playbook

Micro-Changes, Macro-Results

Big-bang rollouts are the graveyard of governance initiatives. They overwhelm, confuse, and create backlash before the benefits can take hold. The smarter path is to implement micro-changes—targeted adjustments that people can absorb, adopt, and normalize quickly. Over time, these micro-changes accumulate into a major transformation, but without the shock that derails adoption. Executives can model this by piloting governance practices in one business area and celebrating visible wins before expanding. Managers can implement micro-changes in how meetings are run, how metrics are reported, or how definitions are shared. Practitioners can make micro-changes in how they log issues, document knowledge, or use tools already at their disposal. Each small step builds confidence and reduces the fear that governance means massive upheaval.

The beauty of micro-changes is their compounding effect. Each successful step reinforces the credibility of the overall initiative. Resistance lowers, trust rises, and momentum builds naturally. What felt like "one more project" starts to feel like an integrated part of how the organization works.

Macro-results—faster project delivery, trusted AI models, reduced compliance risk—eventually become undeniable. But they didn't come from forcing the organization to leap in a single bound. They came from walking steadily, deliberately, one small step at a time.

Embedding Change Leaders

Change doesn't scale because of a single executive sponsor or a central governance team. It scales because leaders are embedded throughout the organization—champions who carry the message, model the behaviors, and influence peers in ways that corporate memos never can. These embedded leaders create credibility by living the change in their daily work.

Executives should invest in identifying these champions, not as formal titles but as trusted voices in each domain. Managers should nurture them by giving them recognition, resources, and platforms to share their successes. Practitioners should be encouraged to step into leadership informally, showing colleagues how small shifts improve results without waiting for permission from above.

Embedding change leaders also creates resilience. When leadership shifts, budgets tighten, or priorities change, embedded champions sustain momentum. Their influence doesn't depend on organizational charts. It depends on relationships, trust, and the daily credibility of their actions.

When change leaders are visible and distributed, governance becomes less of a centralized push and more of a grassroots movement.

Theory is essential, but leaders and practitioners ultimately want to know how change looks when it's lived day-to-day. In practice, change management as a catalyst means embedding adoption into the workflow—not treating it as a separate initiative. It focuses on micro-successes, storytelling, and distributed leadership that make governance and literacy part of the organization's DNA. Table 4 illustrates how change can be embedded into standard organizational practices to reduce resistance and accelerate results.

Area of Practice	Without Managed Change	With Catalyst[3] Change Embedded
Project Rollouts	Staff blindsided, pushback	Early involvement, expectations set
Governance Adoption	Seen as an extra burden	Embedded into roles, natural fit
Training and Learning	One-off, forgettable sessions	Ongoing, tied to daily work
Leadership Engagement	Absent except at launch	Continuous reinforcement by champions
Cultural Alignment	Fragmented, skeptical	Shared stories, collective ownership

Table 4: Organizational Practice Comparison
Without Managed Change Versus With Catalyst[3] Embedded

Storytelling the Change

Data governance lives and dies by the stories people tell. If the story is, "this is slowing us down," adoption stalls. If the story is, "this helped us avoid disaster," adoption flourishes. Storytelling is not fluff—it's the mechanism by which abstract initiatives become tangible and relevant.

Executives can share stories about risks avoided, opportunities seized, and trust gained through effective governance. Managers can tell stories about team wins—how consistent definitions saved hours, or how a governed report prevented a costly mistake. Practitioners can share stories about their own frustrations that have been resolved or their ability to contribute meaningfully with better data access. Each story reinforces why governance and change matter, and each creates a ripple of motivation across the organization.

Good stories don't need to be dramatic.
They need to be relatable.

They need to reflect the pain people actually feel and the relief they want. The best stories are grounded in business outcomes—more accurate forecasts, smoother audits, more reliable AI predictions—and told in language that resonates with business users, not just data professionals.

When stories circulate widely, they normalize change. They shift governance from something abstract into something lived. And once people are repeating stories about the value of governance, the cultural tide has turned. The change has taken root.

Why Change Management Matters

Change is not optional in today's business climate—but unmanaged change is costly. Governance succeeds only when change is understood, respected, and embedded. These reasons demonstrate why change management is not a "soft skill," but a central force in accelerating the adoption of governance.

- **Resistance Reveals Priorities**: Pushback isn't random—it shows where people feel threatened, overloaded, or confused. Instead of treating resistance as failure, practitioners can mine it for insight. Managers can respond by clarifying value. Executives can adjust expectations. Resistance reveals where the organization cares most, making it a roadmap for adoption.

- **Adoption Requires Psychology**: People don't change because they're told to; they change when it makes sense to them. Adoption requires an understanding of identity, fairness, and control. Practitioners need ownership. Managers need clarity. Executives need proof. When adoption psychology is respected, governance shifts from imposed to embraced.

- **Small Wins Build Momentum**: Macro-changes overwhelm. Micro-changes reassure. Practitioners see quick improvements, managers see visible progress, and executives see measurable results. Each win builds confidence that governance isn't just another fad. Momentum is built not by one big success, but by many small ones.

- **Change Leaders Multiply Impact**: One executive sponsor isn't enough. Change sticks when embedded leaders carry it throughout the business. Practitioners influence peers, managers reinforce behaviors, and executives amplify the message. Distributed leadership multiplies the impact of governance efforts.

- **Stories Shape Belief**: People believe stories more than policies. A manager telling a story of avoided rework or a practitioner describing a resolved issue resonates more than a slide deck. Stories normalize change, reduce skepticism, and create cultural buy-in. Executives, managers, and practitioners must all become storytellers.

Ways to Apply Change as a Catalyst

Artifacts to Consider Building

Applying change as a catalyst is about making progress feel achievable, sustainable, and even energizing for the people involved. Instead of overwhelming teams with sweeping initiatives, practitioners can create artifacts that capture resistance, highlight small wins, and empower champions across the organization. These artifacts help transform change management from a reactive process into a proactive accelerator, making governance and literacy easier to adopt and sustain. The following list provides examples of artifacts that can potentially help embed change in practical and impactful ways.

1. Resistance Insight Checklist

Practitioners often view resistance as something to be eliminated, when in reality, it provides insight into where people feel threatened, overloaded, or left out. A **Resistance Insight Checklist** provides practitioners with a structured approach to document resistance, categorize it (by fear, workload, or mistrust), and link it to opportunities for engagement. This shifts the conversation from "How do we stop resistance?" to "What is this resistance telling us?"

By using the checklist consistently, practitioners can show executives and managers that resistance is a map of priorities, not an obstacle to progress. It reframes pushback as an energy source that, if redirected, accelerates adoption. Instead of seeing resistance as failure, organizations see it as proof that people care—and as guidance on how to engage them effectively.

2. Adoption Psychology Plan

An **Adoption Psychology Plan** outlines how governance-related change will be introduced, not just from a process standpoint, but from a human standpoint. It addresses identity ("What does this mean for my role?"), fairness ("Why is this change happening?"), and control ("How much say do I have?"). By planning around these psychological drivers, practitioners can build confidence that change will stick.

This plan is invaluable for executives and managers because it connects governance adoption to leadership empathy. Instead of mandating compliance, leaders can use the plan to frame governance as a fair, inclusive, and empowering shift. Practitioners can position themselves as change partners who anticipate fears and provide reassurance. The result is adoption that feels owned rather than imposed.

3. Momentum Map

Momentum doesn't come from one large initiative; it comes from a series of small wins that build trust and belief. A **Momentum Map** provides practitioners with a simple visual or table showing which wins will be targeted first, how they will be communicated, and how each win builds toward the next. It breaks governance into bite-sized, confidence-building stages.

For executives and managers, the Momentum Map demonstrates that governance is not an all-or-nothing initiative. It creates a clear path of micro-successes that can be celebrated and shared as proof of progress. Practitioners benefit because it gives them a concrete plan for building adoption over time, ensuring momentum isn't left to chance but becomes a designed accelerator.

---

*See how to develop and use this artifact
in the Field Guide at the end of the book.*

---

4. Storytelling Narrative Guide

Change doesn't stick because of policies—it sticks because of stories. A **Storytelling Narrative Guide** provides practitioners with a set of prompts, formats, and examples of how to capture and share real governance success stories. These could include stories of reduced rework, avoided risk, or faster decisions that directly benefited the business.

This guide becomes an amplifier for change. Executives can use it to reinforce strategy in town halls, managers can use it to motivate teams, and practitioners can use it to prove governance value to peers. By institutionalizing stories as a communication tool, governance moves from abstract concepts to lived experiences. Narratives spread faster than policy documents—and they create the culture shift that accelerates adoption.

Actions to Take

Change without drama, resistance as energy, and adoption rooted in psychology—these ideas shift change from an obstacle into an accelerator. But without action, they remain abstract. To make governance stick, change must be managed deliberately, empathetically, and sustainably.

Start by embracing resistance instead of fighting it. Resistance isn't a barrier; it's a signal. When people push back, they're showing you where clarity or reassurance is needed. Treating resistance as energy transforms skeptics into allies. It turns disruption into engagement.

Adoption happens when people feel competent, autonomous, and included. Executives can model adoption by using governed data in their own decisions. Managers can model adoption by listening to feedback and reinforcing new behaviors. Practitioners can model adoption by making small, daily shifts in how they work with data.

Change management as a catalyst isn't about programs. It's about culture. Embed champions, tell stories, and celebrate micro-changes that accumulate into transformation. That's how you accelerate adoption without overwhelming people.

Immediate Actionable Steps

1. Reframe one resistance point in your organization as useful feedback and act on it.

2. Pilot a micro-change in one team and celebrate its results visibly.

3. Identify at least one embedded change leader and give them a platform to share successes.

4. Capture and share a story that demonstrates how governance improved an outcome.

5. Build adoption metrics that measure engagement and sustainability, not just compliance.

FOUR

Data Fluency as a Catalyst

Part A: Theory

Beyond Training—Building Fluency

Most organizations think they're addressing data literacy when they roll out a set of training courses. A few sessions, some slides, maybe a certification badge, and they call it progress. But training is not the same as fluency. Training teaches concepts; fluency builds confidence. Training can check a box, fluency changes behavior. If governance and change management are the structure and process, fluency is the human capacity that makes those structures usable. Without fluency, the other catalysts stall. For executives, fluency (often stated as literacy) isn't about making everyone into data scientists. It's about ensuring every leader can interpret, question, and apply data with enough confidence to make smarter decisions. For managers, fluency is about reducing reliance on bottlenecks—so they don't need to wait weeks for a specialized report but can understand and trust the data in front of them. For practitioners, fluency means the difference between struggling in silence and being able to make meaningful contributions to problem-solving and innovation.

When organizations focus on fluency, they stop treating data as a foreign language. Instead, data becomes an integral part of everyday communication—a shared vocabulary that facilitates collaboration and strengthens decision-making. And just like any language, fluency isn't built in a classroom alone. It's built in daily practice, reinforced in context, and applied where it matters most: in the decisions people make every day.

In the world of data governance, training is often seen as the solution. But while training is a great starting point, it's only the first step. Building fluency—where data is understood, spoken, and used by all—is what makes governance sustainable. Table 5 contrasts traditional approaches to data literacy, which treat it as a one-off event, with the Non-Invasive approach, which embeds fluency into the daily workflow, making data accessible and actionable for everyone, regardless of their technical expertise.

Dimension	Traditional Data Literacy (Training Only)	Catalyst³ Fluency (Embedded Approach)
Scope	Short-term, isolated training sessions	Ongoing, integrated into daily work
Ownership	Relies on a few experts	Distributed across all roles
Sustainability	Forgotten after training ends	Built into workflows and processes
Engagement	Low, often compliance-driven	High, as part of organizational culture
Impact	Limited to a few tasks	Spans across decision-making, operations, and strategy

Table 5: Training Only Versus Catalyst³ Fluency
Implementation Comparison

Speaking the Common Language of Data

One of the most underestimated challenges in organizations is the language barrier that exists between technical teams and business teams. IT professionals might discuss schemas, APIs, or pipelines, while business leaders focus on revenue, risk, and customer satisfaction. Both groups are right in their own terms—but when they can't translate for each other, governance breaks down.

Data fluency bridges the business/IT divide by creating a common language.

Executives benefit from this common language when strategy discussions stop being derailed by debates over definitions and start focusing on actions. Managers benefit when their teams can align on what a metric really means and avoid wasting hours reconciling reports. Practitioners benefit when they are not excluded from conversations due to jargon but instead feel empowered to contribute to dialogue across disciplines. A shared language makes governance tangible rather than theoretical.

This isn't about simplifying things. It's about raising everyone to a baseline where conversations are inclusive, accurate, and productive. The shared language doesn't eliminate the complexity of data, but it makes that complexity navigable. Once people are fluent enough to converse about data in meaningful terms, the organization stops tripping over translation problems and starts accelerating toward outcomes.

Fluency Fuels Decision-Making

Every organization claims to make "data-driven decisions." The reality? Many people still rely on their gut instinct, hierarchy, or whichever report came up first. Data fluency is what makes "data-driven" more than a slogan. Fluency ensures that when decisions are made, they are made with understanding, context, and confidence. Without it, organizations risk decisions that are either paralyzed by confusion or misled by misinformation.

Executives rely on fluency and literacy to avoid being swayed by flashy dashboards that lack substance. They need to ask the right questions: "Where did this data come from? How is it defined? What assumptions are baked in?" Managers rely on literacy to strike a balance between speed and accuracy, ensuring that day-to-day operational decisions are informed and consistent. Practitioners rely on fluency to incorporate data into their workflow, rather than viewing it as a task for someone else.

When fluency spreads across the organization, decision-making becomes sharper and more resilient. AI projects are trusted because people understand how they're fed. Reports are actionable because definitions are shared. Innovation flourishes because people have the confidence to explore data, rather than fear it. Fluency is not a side project—it's the accelerant that turns governance and change into sustainable results.

Part B: Practice and Playbook

Mapping Fluency Levels

The first step to improving fluency is knowing where you are. Too often, organizations assume everyone has the same level of data comfort, but fluency varies widely across roles and individuals. Mapping fluency levels means assessing not only technical skills but also confidence, language, and behaviors. Some people may be highly analytical but struggle to communicate their results effectively. Others may be skeptical of data altogether. Knowing these distinctions matters.

Executives benefit from understanding fluency levels because it helps them target their investments effectively. Managers benefit because it allows them to tailor coaching and team development. Practitioners benefit because it ensures they aren't thrown into situations where expectations exceed their readiness. A clear map transforms fluency and literacy from a vague aspiration into a measurable and actionable initiative.

When fluency is mapped, the organization gains a baseline. From there, programs can be tailored to consistently raise capabilities across the board, ensuring that no group is left behind. It's not about creating uniform experts—it's about ensuring everyone is fluent enough to participate.

Raising the Baseline, Not the Ceiling

One of the traps organizations fall into is aiming to create a handful of superstars while ignoring the broader base. The data scientists, power users, or early adopters get all the attention, while the average employee is left struggling. This creates dependency on a few experts and limits scalability. The smarter strategy is to raise the baseline.

Executives should focus on ensuring that every leader can read, interpret, and question data. Managers should ensure their teams can collaborate around data without bottlenecks. Practitioners should have just enough fluency to feel comfortable using data in their day-to-day work.

---

*Raising the baseline ensures governance is inclusive, **not elitist**.*

When everyone is elevated to a minimum standard of fluency, the organization becomes more agile and resilient. Innovation no longer bottlenecks at the hands of a few experts. Instead, it spreads naturally because everyone has the baseline capability to engage. Governance gains traction because people feel enabled rather than excluded.

Programs That Stick

Many fluency programs fail because they are designed as one-time events. People attend, learn some new terms, and promptly forget them. Programs that stick are built into the workflow. They use real data, relevant to people's roles, and reinforce learning in small, repeatable doses. The most effective programs make fluency feel useful immediately, not like homework for later.

Executives can make programs stick by visibly participating—showing that fluency matters at the top, not just the bottom. Managers can make programs stick by connecting learning directly to team priorities, whether it's a sales pipeline, a compliance report, or a customer service metric. Practitioners can make programs stick by practicing fluency daily—asking questions, challenging assumptions, and applying lessons in their own work.

When fluency programs are designed to stick, they become self-reinforcing. The more people use what they've learned, the more they see the benefits. Over time, fluency becomes culture. And once it's culture, governance and change management don't just have participants. They have partners.

Theory suggests the need for fluency; practice demonstrates how to develop it across the organization. In Part B, we examined how data fluency can be integrated into business processes, making it a core skill that employees utilize to make informed decisions. Table 6 helps illustrate the shift from sporadic data training to widespread fluency, making the learning journey more embedded and sustainable within teams and departments.

Area of Practice	Without Embedded Fluency	With Data Literacy Embedded
Onboarding	Data skills were introduced as an afterthought	Data fluency is integrated from day one
Decision-Making	Driven by gut feeling or siloed information	Data is central to every decision-making process
Collaboration	Misunderstandings due to inconsistent language	Shared understanding through common data language
Risk Management	Data is not trusted; decisions are reactive	Data is trusted and used proactively in risk management
Strategic Alignment	Strategy disconnected from data insights	Data fluency ensures strategies are data-driven and aligned

Table 6: Practice Comparison
Without Versus With Embedded Fluency

Why Fluency Fuels Governance

Data fluency is the multiplier that makes governance and change management stick. Without fluency, governance becomes abstract and adoption collapses. Here's why building fluency is not optional, but essential:

- **Shared Language Breaks Barriers**: Executives, managers, and practitioners often speak different dialects of data. Without a shared language, collaboration stalls. Fluency provides that language, enabling faster, clearer communication across levels.

- **Confidence Drives Participation**: Practitioners hesitate to engage when they feel out of their depth. Managers hesitate to act when they're unsure of data. Executives hesitate to invest when they doubt outcomes. Fluency builds confidence, and confidence drives participation.

- **Baseline Matters More Than Expertise**: Governance collapses when only a handful of experts understand the data. Raising the baseline across the organization ensures everyone can participate. Experts will still lead, but fluency ensures that no one is left behind.

- **Fluency Improves Decisions**: Data-driven decisions aren't made when people don't trust themselves to interpret data. Fluency ensures executives ask sharper questions, managers validate assumptions, and practitioners apply insights accurately.

- **Programs Stick When Practical**: One-off training doesn't change behavior. Programs tied to real data and daily work create fluency that sticks. When governance and literacy are integrated, fluency accelerates adoption naturally.

Ways to Apply Fluency as a Catalyst

Artifacts to Consider Building

Applying fluency as a catalyst means moving beyond one-time training sessions and instead creating tools and practices that embed the discipline into everyday work. The right artifacts make data less intimidating and more accessible, helping people across all levels of the organization develop the confidence and shared language they need to fully participate in data-driven decision-making. The following list highlights examples of artifacts that can potentially transform fluency from a concept into a lived capability, ensuring it accelerates collaboration and trust across the enterprise.

1. Shared Language Glossary Template

One of the simplest but most impactful deliverables is a **Shared Language Glossary Template**. This provides a structured format where practitioners can capture business terms, their definitions, and ownership. It doesn't need to be an extensive, complex data dictionary— it's a lightweight, business-friendly glossary that can evolve over time.

This tool is critical because executives, managers, and practitioners all speak different dialects of data. The glossary template bridges those gaps, ensuring that a "customer," a "transaction," or a "risk" means the same thing across departments. When people stop arguing about definitions and start trusting each other's data, collaboration accelerates.

See how to develop and use this artifact
in the Field Guide at the end of the book.

---

2. Data Confidence Self-Assessment Checklist

Practitioners can help their colleagues measure their own comfort level with data by creating a **Data Confidence Self-Assessment Checklist**. This checklist can ask simple, non-threatening questions, such as "Do I know where this data came from?" or "Do I feel confident presenting this metric to leadership?"

The value here is that it makes confidence visible. Executives can see where their teams feel strong and where support is needed. Managers can identify gaps without judgment, and practitioners can initiate conversations about the type of support, literacy programs, or governance interventions that are required. By normalizing confidence checks, organizations empower people to participate more fully in data-driven decisions.

3. Baseline Fluency Development Plan

A **Baseline Fluency Development Plan** helps practitioners document the current state of literacy or fluency across roles and outline how to raise the floor without aiming for unrealistic expertise. It identifies critical skills, such as interpreting dashboards, questioning data sources, or understanding data lineage, and provides a path for gradually embedding them.

This plan resonates with executives and managers because it shows that fluency isn't about turning everyone into data scientists. It's about ensuring no one is left behind. By raising the baseline, practitioners ensure governance is sustainable and scalable. The plan becomes proof that fluency is not a training event, but a cultural investment.

4. Decision-Making Fluency Model

A **Decision-Making Fluency Model** maps how decisions are made today, highlighting where poor data understanding slows down the process or creates risk. The model then illustrates what fluent decision-making looks like—where executives ask sharper questions, managers validate assumptions, and practitioners apply insights responsibly.

For leadership, this model illustrates how literacy and fluency directly influences the speed and quality of decision-making. For practitioners, it provides a structured way to demonstrate the value of building fluency, not as an abstract goal but as a tangible accelerator of business performance. The model is a communication tool that makes literacy measurable and relevant.

5. Practical Training and Application Outline

Training only sticks when tied to real-world needs. A **Practical Training and Application Outline** ensures fluency efforts are embedded into daily work. This deliverable outlines the topics that should be addressed (definitions, dashboards, risk awareness), the most effective formats (workshops, office hours, peer mentoring), and how lessons are reinforced in actual projects.

This outline is powerful because it reframes literacy and fluency from "one more training session" into a driver of productivity. Practitioners can use it to show managers and executives that these programs don't take time away from work—they enhance it. By linking learning to outcomes, this outline ensures fluency is seen as a catalyst, not a distraction.

Actions to Take

Fluency, not training, is the goal. Shared language, not jargon, is the bridge. Confidence in decision-making, not dependence on specialists, is the outcome. Data fluency as a catalyst means ensuring that everyone—not just analysts—can participate in governed data.

Start by mapping fluency levels honestly. Don't assume people know more than they do, but don't underestimate their potential either. Raising the baseline for the entire organization creates inclusion. The goal isn't to make everyone an expert—it's to make everyone fluent enough to participate.

Fluency fuels decision-making at every level. Executives can question data with confidence. Managers can collaborate without bottlenecks. Practitioners can apply data in their daily work instead of waiting for handoffs. Once fluency becomes culture, governance has a partner that amplifies its impact.

Build literacy into real work, use real data,
and reinforce it often.
As fluency grows, governance naturally accelerates.

Immediate Actionable Steps

1. Conduct a simple assessment of data fluency levels across your team or organization.
2. Identify one shared definition or concept that can reduce confusion and teach it broadly.
3. Build one fluency activity into a real project (e.g., ask leaders to interpret a dataset).
4. Focus on raising the baseline by targeting everyday users, not just advanced analysts.
5. Create an ongoing rhythm of reinforcement—small, frequent fluency moments, not one-off training.

FIVE

Changing the Narrative of Data Governance

Stop Selling Pain, Start Selling Value

One of the biggest reasons governance fails to take hold is the way it's sold. Too often, the message to executives focuses on avoiding fines, passing audits, or mitigating risk. To managers, it's about compliance. To practitioners, it's about the rules they must follow. In other words, governance is positioned as a painkiller—necessary but unpleasant. The problem with painkillers is that people only reach for them when the pain is acute, and the moment the pain subsides, the motivation to continue fades.

The narrative must shift to value.

Executives need to hear how governance accelerates AI adoption, speeds decision-making, and increases return on technology investments. Managers need to hear how governance reduces rework, eliminates firefighting, and improves team efficiency. Practitioners need to hear how governance simplifies their daily work, removes uncertainty, and validates their contributions. When governance is framed as an accelerator rather than a constraint, it stops being something people tolerate and starts being something they champion.

The key is specificity. Telling people "governance is good for you" is meaningless. Showing an executive how governance can reduce the time-to-market for a new product by weeks is persuasive. Demonstrating to a manager how it saves 20% of their team's time on report reconciliation is impactful. Highlighting for a practitioner how it prevents them from being blamed for inconsistent data is powerful. Specific, relatable value is what makes governance relevant.

Once governance is tied to measurable value, the conversation changes. Instead of executives asking, "Do we really need this?" they start asking, "How do we get more of this?" Instead of managers feeling burdened, they feel supported. Instead of practitioners rolling their eyes, they lean in. That's when governance stops being a painkiller and becomes a performance enhancer—something people reach for because it helps them win.

When it comes to data governance, most organizations approach the conversation through a lens of risk and compliance—they focus on the pain of failure, fines, and audits. While those are real concerns, this narrative fails to inspire action or gain buy-in from leadership. A shift is needed: instead of selling governance as a necessary evil, we need to frame it as an enabler of business value, innovation, and speed. Table 7 highlights how governance is reframed from pain avoidance to value creation, ensuring that the message resonates with both executives and practitioners.

Narrative	Old Perception	New Data Catalyst[3] Framing	Impact of Reframing
Compliance	Costly, mandatory, painful	Safeguard for speed and AI trust	Executives see advantage
Rules	Burdensome, disruptive	Guardrails for clarity	Managers see efficiency
Extra Work	Add-on tasks for staff	Embedded in daily roles	Practitioners see value
Enforcement	Fear-driven compliance	Catalyst for acceleration	Builds long-term culture

Table 7: Narrative Reframing

Enablement Hints at Passiveness

In recent years, many organizations have tried to rebrand governance as "enablement." The intent is good: to soften the image of governance as something rigid and controlling. However, the word "enablement" presents its own challenges. It suggests passivity—as though governance is standing on the sidelines, offering tools and cheerleading, but not really driving outcomes. Enablement is essential, but it isn't enough. Organizations don't just need data to be "enabled." They need it to be accelerated.

Executives aren't looking for enablement. They're looking for performance. They aim to explore how governance can create a market advantage, reduce costs, and mitigate risks associated with AI investments. Managers aren't looking for enablement either. They want support that makes their teams more effective, not handouts that leave them figuring out the rest. Practitioners don't want to be "enabled" in a vague sense. They want governance that makes their jobs easier today, not someday.

> *When governance is framed as passive enablement,*
> *it risks being dismissed as a "nice to have."*

The difference is in posture. Enablement is reactive—waiting for someone to ask for help. Catalyst is proactive—driving change, sparking energy, and creating visible wins without being asked. That difference matters because organizations in the world of AI and real-time decisions don't have the luxury of slow, reactive governance.

Reframing governance from an enabler to a catalyst requires a shift in storytelling, metrics, and behavior. Show executives how governance fuels growth. Show managers how it reduces friction. Show practitioners how it lightens their workload. When the message shifts from passive to active, governance stops being something that quietly supports from the background. It becomes something that actively propels the organization forward.

Governance as Catalyst, Not Enforcer

The traditional metaphor for governance is enforcement—rules, policies, standards—enforced from above, with compliance as the measure of success. But enforcement only works if people fear the consequences of breaking the rules. The moment attention drifts, compliance falters. Enforcement breeds short-term obedience, not long-term engagement. In a world where speed, innovation, and trust are paramount, enforcement alone is unsustainable.

Governance as a catalyst flips the metaphor. Instead of focusing on what people *can't* do, it focuses on what they *can* do better, faster, and with more confidence. Executives view governance not as a watchdog, but as a turbocharger—ensuring that data-driven strategies are executed with fewer risks and more reliable outcomes. Managers see governance not as a set of handcuffs, but as a support system that helps their teams perform more efficiently. Practitioners view governance not as policing, but as scaffolding—providing them with the clarity and guardrails to build with confidence.

Catalysts don't slow reactions down. They speed them up. That's exactly the role governance must play in the age of AI and analytics. It accelerates adoption by making data trustworthy. It accelerates execution by clarifying roles. It accelerates innovation by reducing uncertainty. When governance is reframed as a catalyst, it becomes something people *want* to participate in, not something they're forced to comply with.

Making this shift isn't just a communications exercise. It's a cultural shift. Governance teams must stop measuring themselves by how many policies they've written or how many audits they've passed. They must start measuring how much faster projects go, how much more confidently decisions are made, and how much more reliable AI models become. That's the difference between enforcer and catalyst. And that's the difference between governance that survives and governance that thrives.

Rebranding Data Governance for the AI Era

AI is transforming how organizations approach data. Suddenly, it's not just about reports and dashboards—it's about predictive models, automated decisions, and generative systems that can create content, code, and insights on demand. In this new world, the old narrative of governance as compliance is dangerously outdated. AI doesn't just need governed data—it demands it. Without governance, AI amplifies errors, accelerates bias, and magnifies risk at scale.

For executives, the AI era reframes governance as essential to trust. Investors, regulators, and customers all want assurance that AI outputs can be trusted. Without governance, that trust evaporates, and so does competitive advantage. For managers, the AI era makes governance the foundation of operational resilience. Their teams can't afford to chase down untrustworthy inputs when AI is making decisions in real time.

For practitioners, the AI era makes governance a shield—protecting them from being blamed when AI misfires due to flawed or biased data.

Rebranding governance for AI isn't just about slogans. It's about aligning governance narratives with AI priorities. Show how governance reduces AI risk, ensures fairness, and improves model performance. Demonstrate how governance enables the responsible scaling of AI adoption. Show how governance prevents the nightmare scenarios of biased recommendations, failed audits, and reputational damage. When governance is tied to AI success, it stops being a compliance cost and starts being a competitive advantage.

The AI era presents governance with an opportunity for reinvention. Instead of being seen as the department of "no," governance can be positioned as the department of "yes, and here's how we do it safely." This is the moment to rebrand governance not as a backward-looking compliance activity, but as a forward-looking accelerator of trustworthy AI. Organizations that seize this narrative will lead. Those that don't risk falling behind—or worse, falling apart under the weight of ungoverned AI.

Why the Story Shapes Governance Success

The story told about governance often determines its fate. If the narrative is negative, governance stalls. If it is catalytic, governance thrives. Here's why words, stories, and framing matter more than most practitioners realize:

- **Words Influence Perception**: Executives hear "compliance" and think cost. Managers hear "rules" and think disruption. Practitioners hear "governance" and think extra work. Words shape perception, which shapes behavior. Choosing catalytic language reframes governance as a means of acceleration.

- **Value Sells, Pain Doesn't**: Selling governance as pain avoidance doesn't inspire action. Selling it as value creation does. Executives buy speed and advantage. Managers buy efficiency. Practitioners buy clarity. Selling value ensures governance gets attention.

- **Enforcer Narratives Breed Fear**: Positioning governance as enforcement invites avoidance and resistance. Framing it as a catalyst invites contribution. Fear drives compliance only temporarily; contribution sustains culture.

- **AI Raises the Stakes**: In the AI era, narratives about governance matter more than ever. If governance is perceived as optional, AI risks multiply. If governance is framed as essential, AI becomes trusted and scalable. The story we tell shapes the systems we build.

- **Stories Spread Faster Than Policies**: A good story about governance accelerating success spreads faster than any policy document. Managers repeat it, practitioners share it, executives cite it. Stories embed governance into culture.

Ways to Change the Governance Narrative

Artifacts to Consider Building

Changing the governance narrative requires more than just new language—it requires visible tools and examples that reinforce the message. By creating the right artifacts, practitioners can shift perceptions from governance as enforcement to governance as an accelerator of value. These artifacts help leaders and teams consistently tell the new story, spread it across the organization, and embed it into culture. The following list highlights artifacts that can potentially help reshape the narrative and make the value of governance impossible to ignore.

1. Narrative Reframing Playbook

A **Narrative Reframing Playbook** equips practitioners with a structured set of "old story versus new story" reframes. For example, the old story is that governance *is about control. The new story is that governance accelerates decisions by clarifying accountability.* The guide can be built as a simple one-pager with three columns: *Myth / Old Perception, Reframe, and Business Value.*

This tool is powerful because it helps executives, managers, and practitioners consistently tell the new story. Instead of each leader inventing their own pitch, everyone can pull from a unified set of messages. Over time, repetition solidifies the narrative shift, ensuring that governance is viewed as a catalyst rather than a constraint.

---

*See how to develop and use this artifact
in the Field Guide at the end of the book.*

---

2. Executive Storytelling Toolkit

Executives are the amplifiers of narrative. A **Storytelling Toolkit** provides them with short, relatable governance success stories they can use in speeches, team meetings, or board updates. Each story should focus on a real win: reduced rework, avoided risk, or faster AI deployment. The toolkit should also provide prompts for leaders to craft their own narratives.

The value here is that stories spread faster than policies. By equipping leaders with ready-made narratives, practitioners ensure the new message about governance cascades naturally across the organization. This shifts culture not by force, but by storytelling—a form of influence executives already know how to wield.

3. Pain-to-Value Communication Map

Governance has often been sold as a way to *avoid pain*—preventing fines, failures, or conflicts. A **Pain-to-Value Communication Map** helps practitioners flip that narrative. It lists common governance pain points ("audit risk," "duplicate reports," "slow compliance") and provides corresponding value-oriented reframes ("audit readiness," "single version of truth," "faster compliance through trust").

This communication map ensures governance conversations move from fear-based messaging to value-based selling. Executives prefer advantage over avoidance, managers respond to efficiency, and practitioners engage with clarity. With this deliverable, governance is no longer viewed as a defensive mechanism, but rather as a business accelerator.

4. Catalyst³ Narrative Model

A **Catalyst³ Narrative Model** is a simple diagram or template that illustrates how governance, change management, and literacy work together to reframe the story. Alone, governance is perceived as enforcement. Change management reframes it as adoption. Literacy reframes it as empowerment. Together, the three disciplines become a catalyst for acceleration.

This model helps practitioners communicate why narrative matters and how it shifts when Catalyst³ is applied. It gives leaders a mental model they can quickly grasp and repeat. Instead of discussing governance as an obligation, they begin talking about it as an enabler—precisely the kind of cultural pivot that changes the game.

Actions to Take

If governance is framed as pain, people resist. If it's framed as enablement, people tend to ignore it. If it's framed as a catalyst, people lean in. Changing the narrative is one of the most powerful levers at your disposal.

Start by selling value instead of pain. Don't talk about governance as a cost or an obligation. Talk about it as acceleration—as the enabler of faster insights, safer AI, and more intelligent decisions. Executives respond to speed. Managers respond to efficiency. Practitioners respond to clarity. Tailor your story to each.

Narratives shape culture.

Stop using passive language like "enablement" and start using active language like "acceleration" and "catalyst." Words matter. They carry weight and influence perception. In the AI era, governance must be framed as the safeguard that enables innovation to scale safely.

Changing the narrative isn't a one-time rebrand. It's a continuous act of storytelling, reinforcement, and proof. The more stories you tell, the more the narrative shifts. The more the narrative shifts, the easier governance becomes.

Immediate Actionable Steps

1. Replace one compliance-focused governance message with a value-focused one.

2. Develop a short elevator pitch that positions governance as a catalyst.

3. Collect and share at least one governance story per quarter that highlights acceleration.

4. Stop using passive terms like "enablement" in your communications and adopt active ones.

5. Connect governance explicitly to your organization's AI strategy in leadership discussions.

Six

Calls to Action
Across the Organization

Executives—Champion the Spark

Executives set the tone for whether governance, change, and fluency are treated as side projects or as essential accelerators of business success. When leaders treat governance as optional, the organization tends to follow suit. But when leaders consistently champion it, tie it to strategy, and model its use in their own decisions, the spark catches fire across the enterprise. Championing the spark doesn't require technical expertise—it requires visible commitment and steady reinforcement.

A practical call to action for executives is to integrate governance into strategic conversations. Don't just ask "What's the ROI on this AI platform?" Ask, "How will we trust the outputs of this AI platform?" Require governance to be embedded into every significant data-related initiative, from digital transformation to risk management. The message to the organization should be clear: governance isn't a compliance cost; it's a performance enabler.

Finally, executives must become storytellers. Share wins publicly, highlight avoided risks, and praise teams who embrace governance, literacy, and change. When the top of the organization demonstrates excitement and commitment, it gives everyone else permission—and motivation—to view governance as something that strengthens the business, not hinders it.

Managers—Operationalize the Energy

Managers are the linchpin between executive vision and daily execution. They translate strategy into reality, and they're often the ones who feel the tension between ambitious goals and limited resources. That's why their call to action is to operationalize the energy created by governance, change, and literacy. Without managers carrying the torch, executive enthusiasm never makes it past the boardroom.

Managers can operationalize by embedding governance checkpoints into their team's workflow—not as roadblocks, but as accelerators that prevent rework later. They should model data fluency in their team meetings, reinforce shared definitions, and encourage team members to raise concerns early. By normalizing these behaviors, managers reduce the friction that often stalls governance programs.

Managers should also act as multipliers of trust. When their teams see that managers rely on governed data to make decisions, confidence spreads. When they see their managers listening to resistance and turning it into feedback, adoption strengthens. And when managers connect governance to tangible team outcomes, such as faster reports, fewer escalations, and smoother audits, energy builds and sustains itself.

Practitioners—Live the Change Daily

Practitioners are the heartbeat of governance because they're the ones defining, producing, and using data every single day. Their call to action is to live the change daily—not by taking on more work, but by formalizing the work they already do. Every time a practitioner documents a definition, flags a quality issue, or explains context to a peer, they're contributing to governance. The challenge is to make those contributions deliberate and consistent.

> *Practitioners should adopt the mindset that governance is not someone else's responsibility.*

It's already part of their jobs—the difference is recognizing it, labeling it, and participating in it consciously. By logging issues in shared systems, participating in stewardship discussions, and using the common language of data, practitioners help governance come alive where it matters most: at the point of use.

Their impact is amplified when they share their wins. If a clarified definition saved them hours, tell that story. If a quality issue was resolved quickly because of governance, highlight it to peers. These stories normalize participation and shift the culture from one of compliance to one of contribution. Practitioners don't just live the change—they spread it.

Everyone Else—Be Data-Woke

Not everyone in the organization is an executive, manager, or data practitioner. But everyone interacts with data, whether they realize it or not. The call to action for the broader workforce is simple: be data-woke. Recognize that every click, entry, and decision creates or consumes data that shapes the business.

Governance isn't something happening far away in IT or an analytics department. It's part of the reality of every role.

Being data-woke starts with awareness. Employees should ask basic but powerful questions: "Where did this data come from? Can I trust it? Who owns it?" These questions don't require deep technical skills—they require curiosity and accountability. When people at all levels start asking them, the culture shifts from passive data use to active data stewardship.

Finally, being data-woke means embracing personal accountability. Whether you're in HR entering employee records, in sales updating pipeline opportunities, or in customer service logging interactions, your actions impact data quality, consistency, and trust. When everyone sees their role in governance, the spark of Data Catalyst³ becomes real—and unstoppable.

Why Roles Matter as a Catalyst

Data Catalyst³ only works when every level of the organization participates. Here's why roles matter and why no one can sit on the sidelines:

- **Executives Set the Tone**: Without visible executive sponsorship, governance never scales. Executives' actions and stories model priorities for everyone else. Their tone shapes the culture.
- **Managers Translate Strategy**: Managers bridge the gap between executive vision and practitioner reality. They

operationalize governance, embed literacy and fluency, and manage resistance. Without them, governance stalls.

- **Practitioners Live it Daily**: Governance succeeds or fails at the point of use. Practitioners define, produce, and consume data. If they aren't engaged, governance is abstract.
- **Everyone Else Contributes**: Even those outside formal governance roles touch data every day. Records clerks, sales reps, HR staff—each has a hand in trust. Everyone's role matters.
- **Distributed Ownership Sustains**: When ownership is distributed across executives, managers, practitioners, and everyone else, governance becomes sustainable. No one role carries it alone.

For any governance initiative to succeed, it requires leadership at all levels. Executives must champion the spark—setting the tone and aligning the organization to embrace governance as a strategic enabler. Managers, on the other hand, are responsible for operationalizing that energy, ensuring that the vision is translated into action across the teams. Table 8 clearly differentiates the roles and responsibilities of executives and managers, providing a clear guide for how both groups can act to drive momentum and ensure success.

Audience	Call to Action	Practical First Step	Why It Matters
Executives	Champion the spark	Tie governance to strategy discussions	Sets tone, signals importance
Managers	Operationalize energy	Embed checkpoints in workflows	Reduces rework, builds trust
Practitioners	Live the change daily	Document and share data issues	Makes governance real at the point of use
Everyone Else	Be data-woke	Ask: "Where did this data come from?"	Builds culture of accountability

Table 8: Call to Action Roadmap for Each Level

Actions to Take

Executives, managers, practitioners, and everyone else each have a role to play. Governance fails when it's seen as someone else's job. Data Catalyst³ works only when accountability is distributed and action is tailored to each level.

Executives must sponsor and model. Managers must operationalize and reinforce. Practitioners must live the change daily. Everyone else must recognize their role in governing the data they touch. Each action, small or large, contributes to the cube.

The beauty of Data Catalyst³ is that it doesn't require perfection. It requires participation. Every person who steps up moves the organization forward. And when enough people step up, the shift becomes culture.

The call is not optional. It's essential. Your world demands governed data. The cube provides the framework. The only thing left is your action.

Immediate Actionable Steps

1. Define one action for executives, managers, and practitioners in your organization this quarter.

2. Hold a short session with your leadership team to link Data Catalyst³ to strategic goals.

3. Encourage managers to pilot one Data Catalyst³ principle in their teams immediately.

4. Recognize practitioners who are already contributing and celebrate their role.

5. Launch a campaign to raise data awareness across "everyone else" in the organization.

SEVEN

Pulling It All Together

Cubed in Action

The power of Data Catalyst[3] is best understood not in theory but in practice. Imagine an organization that struggled for years with conflicting reports. Executives had lost patience, managers spent hours reconciling numbers, and practitioners felt invisible. By weaving together governance, change management, and literacy, the organization didn't just fix reports. It built trust. Suddenly, executives made confident decisions without second-guessing. Managers directed resources more effectively. Practitioners saw their work recognized as essential to success. That's Data Catalyst³ in action—three disciplines converging to deliver acceleration, trust, and value.

Stories like these aren't rare. They're happening quietly in organizations that stopped treating governance, change, and literacy as side projects and started treating them as accelerators. An insurance company utilized Data Catalyst³ to establish data trust, unlocking AI adoption across claims. A university applied it to harmonize student data, building confidence in analytics that improved retention strategies. In both cases, governance alone wouldn't have been enough. Change management alone wouldn't have been enough. Literacy or fluency alone wouldn't have been enough. But cubed? It multiplied impact and created lasting results.

Executives who once doubted governance became advocates when they saw outcomes tied to business goals. Managers who once complained about disruption became champions when they saw smoother workflows. Practitioners who once resisted governance became leaders when they realized their contributions mattered. The transformation wasn't in policies or tools. It was in mindset—the recognition that governance, change, and literacy together spark acceleration.

As you reflect on Data Catalyst³, remember this: action is the test. These stories aren't blueprints for perfection; they're proof that momentum builds when people start where they are, apply the principles consistently, and measure outcomes in terms of speed, trust, and adoption. The following case study could be yours.

Lighting the Path Forward

The path forward isn't complicated, but it does require courage. It requires executives to make governance part of their strategic DNA. It requires managers to translate strategy into sustainable practices. It requires practitioners to show up every day, ready to integrate governance into their normal workflow. And it requires everyone else to recognize that their actions with data, big or small, matter more than they realize.

For executives, the call is to demand governance that accelerates value. Don't settle for governance that exists only on paper. Insist on governance that drives adoption, builds trust, and proves ROI. For managers, the call is to embed governance into operations without drama—integrating it into the way work is already done. For practitioners, the call is to raise your voice, share your knowledge, and live the change. And for everyone else, the call is to be curious, be responsible, and be data-woke.

Data Catalyst³ provides a roadmap: governance as the structure, change management as the adoption engine, and fluency as the human multiplier.

Follow it, and you'll discover that data no longer feels like a burden. It feels like the most powerful tool your organization has to succeed. The path isn't linear. There will be resistance, setbacks, and detours. But each step builds momentum, and each success makes the next one easier.

Most importantly, lighting the path forward means refusing to let governance be sidelined as "extra work." The future of your organization, and your AI strategy, depends on governed data. Without it, the risks multiply. With it, the possibilities of where to go expand. This is the moment to step up, ignite the catalyst, and walk the path with confidence.

The Data Catalyst Mindset

At the heart of this book is a simple but profound shift: governance, change, and fluency aren't chores. They're catalysts. They don't slow you down. They speed you up. That mindset is the foundation for a new culture—one where people stop asking, "Why do we need governance?"

and start asking, "How do we get more of it?" Once that shift takes hold, the energy it creates is unstoppable.

Executives with the Data Catalyst³ mindset don't tolerate unreliable data—they demand governance to make it trustworthy. Managers with the Data Catalyst³ mindset don't view resistance as a problem—they use it as a source of energy to guide adoption. Practitioners with the Data Catalyst³ mindset don't feel burdened by governance—they feel empowered to contribute to it. Everyone else with the Data Catalyst³ mindset doesn't treat data as someone else's job—they treat it as a shared asset that requires shared accountability.

Mindset matters because it shapes behavior. When governance is seen as an enforcer, people comply reluctantly. When governance is seen as a catalyst, people contribute enthusiastically. The difference between slow adoption and rapid acceleration is often in how people perceive the work. The Data Catalyst mindset makes governance a source of pride instead of pain.

This mindset belongs to everyone.
It's about believing that data—
when governed non-invasively,
adopted thoughtfully, understood fluently—
can transform.

Why Catalyst³ Actions Can't Wait

Ultimately, the argument for Data Catalyst³ hinges on timing. Governance, change, and fluency are not concepts that can be shelved until the organization is "ready." The truth is that waiting only makes the challenge harder. AI won't slow down, competitors won't pause, and cultures won't sit idle until you decide to act. Every day you delay, the risk grows and the opportunities shrink. Here's why action is not just important but urgent—and why every practitioner, manager, and executive must treat governance as a new priority, not a someday project:

- **AI Won't Wait**: AI is scaling faster than governance. Delay creates risk. Acting now ensures governance supports, rather than chases, AI.

- **Trust is Fragile**: Every governance failure erodes trust, and rebuilding is hard. Acting quickly builds credibility that compounds over time.

- **Competitors are Moving**: Others are already using governed data to gain speed and trust. Inaction leaves you behind. Governance is no longer optional.

- **Culture Sets Permanently**: If governance isn't framed as a catalyst now, it risks being cemented as compliance later. Early actions shape lasting culture.

- **Momentum Multiplies**: Small actions now create momentum that multiplies. Waiting stalls energy. Acting builds acceleration into the DNA of the organization.

The urgency of taking action cannot be overstated. Whether it's AI racing ahead without governance, the erosion of trust, or competitors moving faster, the risks of inaction are profound. Table 9 provides a clear comparison, outlining the critical urgency factors and the risks of waiting versus the tangible benefits of acting now. By addressing these factors with the Catalyst[3] framework, organizations can mitigate risk and seize opportunities that propel them ahead of the competition, ensuring sustainable, data-driven success.

Urgency Factor	Risk of Waiting	Benefit of Acting Now
AI	Models built on ungoverned data	Trustworthy, scalable adoption
Trust	Erodes quickly, slow to rebuild	Credibility compounds with every success
Competitors	Others move ahead with governed data	Competitive edge maintained
Culture	Governance cemented as compliance	Governance cemented as catalyst
Momentum	Energy stalls	Small wins multiply into acceleration

Table 9: The Risk of Waiting on the Data Catalyst³

Compelling Wrap-Up: Share the Message

Now comes the part where I ask you to take what you've read and do something about it. Don't keep Data Catalyst³ to yourself. Share it. Talk about it in your next team meeting. Bring it up in your executive updates. Weave it into conversations about AI, digital transformation, and risk. Your world requires governed data—not governed with heavy hands but governed using the Non-Invasive Data Governance approach. Without it, AI collapses. Transformation stalls. Trust evaporates. With it, everything accelerates.

Executives won't always read books like this. They rely on you to bring the message to them. Be their translator. Show them how Data Catalyst³ ties directly to what they care about: speed, trust, innovation, compliance, and competitive advantage. Don't wait for governance to be assigned as a project. Make it part of every conversation about the future.

The urgency is real. Regulators are tightening. AI is expanding. Customers are expecting transparency. Competitors are moving fast. This is not the time to let governance be optional. This is the time to position it as the accelerator your organization needs. The moment to act is now.

Be the spark that ignites Data Catalyst³.
Become the advocate who makes governance not
just possible but unstoppable.

Actions to Take

This book doesn't end here. It ends when you act. The principles of Data Catalyst³—governance, change, and literacy—are not meant to sit in theory. They're meant to come alive in your organization.

The urgency is real. AI is here. Regulation is tightening. Customers demand trust. Competitors are moving faster. You don't have the luxury of treating governance as optional. Data Catalyst³ is not just a framework. It's a survival guide—and a growth engine.

Your next step is to share this message. Bring it to your executives, your managers, your peers. Don't wait for the perfect time. The time is now. Governance, done the Non-Invasive way, accelerates everything else.

If this book has sparked something in you, don't let it fade. Take the message upward, outward, and forward. Be the catalyst. Multiply the spark. And help your organization unlock the speed, trust, and innovation that only governed data can deliver.

Immediate Actionable Steps

1. Share the core message of Data Catalyst³ with your executive team.
2. Choose one Data Catalyst³ principle to apply immediately in your own role.
3. Tell a story of governance success to influence others' perception.
4. Identify a partner or peer to hold you accountable for action.
5. Commit to being the voice that carries Data Catalyst³ into your organization's culture.

Where to Go to Get Additional Information About The Data Catalyst³

As you reach the end of this part of the book, I hope that you feel both empowered and equipped to bring Data Catalyst³ to life in your organization. But I also know that one book, no matter how detailed, cannot answer every question. Data governance, change management, and data fluency are dynamic disciplines that evolve in tandem with technology, regulation, and culture. If you want to dive deeper into the subjects you've encountered here, I encourage you to explore the many articles, blogs, and resources I've written and shared over the years through conferences, webinars, and professional networks. Many of these are freely available, and all are designed to extend the principles you've read here into actionable next steps.

For those who want to work directly with me and my colleagues, the best place to start is with KIK Consulting and Educational Services. At KIK, we've built a practice around helping organizations formalize governance in a Non-Invasive way, equipping them with proven frameworks, templates, and approaches. Our mission has always been to meet organizations where they are, to respect their culture, and to guide them toward governance that accelerates results without disruption.

KIK Consulting doesn't stand alone. Over the past decade, I've been fortunate to build partnerships with international firms that share the same values and that extend the reach of Non-Invasive Data Governance into their regions and markets. Our friends at Innoscale AG in Germany have digitized the NIDG framework into technology that makes governance accessible and actionable for enterprises worldwide. In South Africa, InfoBluePrint has combined its expertise in data strategy and implementation with NIDG to deliver governance programs across industries. In North America, we've partnered with firms like Innova COE, whose strong roots in change management and data fluency help organizations put NIDG into practice alongside these other critical disciplines. Each of these partnerships demonstrates that governance is not a local concept—it's global, it's universal, and it resonates wherever people need trusted data.

It would be impossible to finish this book without acknowledging the individuals who have influenced me the most in the data space. Their ideas, their work, and their commitment to advancing our field have shaped not only my thinking but the very fabric of what I've shared with you here. Larry English, one of the early pioneers in data quality, showed us that the pursuit of trusted data is a business discipline, not just a technical task. John Ladley, a respected thought leader, consultant, and author, has long been a voice for practical, business-first governance. Gwen Thomas, founder of the Data Governance Institute, paved the way for so many of us by formalizing governance into a discipline and community before most organizations even had a name for it.

I have also been shaped by Danette McGilvray, whose work on data quality and information management consistently emphasized the human dimension of data—a principle very much aligned with the Non-Invasive approach. David Plotkin has made immeasurable contributions through his writing and consulting, demonstrating to organizations how to balance technical rigor with business priorities. And I would be remiss not to mention Peter Aiken, whose academic and practical work has elevated data management as a discipline worthy of executive attention, helping to legitimize roles such as the Chief Data Officer. Each of these leaders has given me—and the community at large—both inspiration and validation. *If I did not mention you above, you probably are part of me and my approach through our interactions over the years and I hope (and expect that) you know who you are.*

Beyond individuals, the community itself has been a constant influence. Through conferences, webinars, professional associations, and collaborative engagements, I've been able to listen, learn, and adapt. Every client I've worked with, every practitioner I've met, has added something to the NIDG story. The truth is that governance has never been about a single voice. It's about a community of professionals, each bringing their own experiences and insights, working together to build a collective understanding of what it means to manage and govern data responsibly.

So, where should you go from here? My suggestion is simple: start where you are. Use the resources you have, lean on the frameworks we've discussed, and don't hesitate to reach out for guidance. Visit the KIK Consulting website, connect with our international partners, and follow the ongoing work being done by the individuals I've named above. The governance community is active and growing, and by engaging with it, you'll find support, ideas, and encouragement for your own Data Catalyst³ journey.

Finally, I leave you with this. The world you are working in now demands governed data. AI has raised the stakes, but the answer remains the same—formalize governance in a way that works with your culture, not against it. The Non-Invasive path is not just a method; it's a movement. And movements thrive when people carry them forward. Take what you've learned here, share it with your executives and colleagues, and be the voice that shifts the narrative. If enough of us do that, the future of governance won't just be about compliance. It will be about trust, acceleration, and unleashing the full potential of people and their data.

The Role AI Played in the Delivery of This Book

It would be hard to write a book about data, governance, change, and fluency in the age of AI without acknowledging the role AI itself played in bringing this book to life. Generative AI tools were instrumental not only in shaping the flow of ideas but also in editing and transforming those ideas into a more polished, accessible narrative. From brainstorming structures and framing concepts to refining my drafts and strengthening clarity, AI served as a true collaborator. While the voice, vision, and substance of the book remain mine, AI provided a layer of support that ensured ideas were organized, refined, and delivered at the speed modern publishing demands.

One of the most striking contributions of AI was the creation of the incredible abstract graphics featured throughout the book. Each section is anchored by a visual that represents its message in a way that words alone could not capture. These designs, although abstract, evoke the spark, structure, and flow of the concepts within Data Catalyst[3], and they were generated with precision and creativity that significantly accelerated the design process. The ability to produce professional, thought-provoking graphics in minutes rather than months is one of the most practical examples of how AI can increase productivity.

AI also provided value in what I like to call the "clean-up" role. Every author knows the challenge of turning raw drafts into smooth, engaging sections that connect with readers at every level—from executives to practitioners. With AI, I was able to iterate more quickly, remove redundancies, and ensure consistency of tone across the entire manuscript. The result is a cleaner, sharper, and more consistent delivery that keeps the focus on the ideas rather than the mechanics of the writing. AI didn't change my message; it amplified it.

The lesson is simple: Generative AI is not a gimmick, nor is it a threat to creativity—it is the wave of the future. Those who learn to use AI wisely will discover that it simplifies their lives and enhances their work productivity. For me, it has been a companion that has accelerated the creation of this book without sacrificing authenticity. For you, it can be the same in your daily work, governance practice, or personal productivity. Learn it, use it, and let it enhance what you already do well. That is the true catalyst that AI represents for all of us.

The Activation and Acceleration Guide

*Sequencing, Routines,
Playbooks,
and Behavioral Guidance*

*The Engine That
Makes the Rest
of the Book Usable.*

The Activation and Acceleration Guide portion of this book is not a recap of the book – it is the **activation engine** that makes the rest of the book usable. The other sections give you the disciplines, the canvases, and the shifts in mindset. But understanding a catalyst is not the same as becoming one. This guide translates everything from concept into movement – showing you how to combine governance, change, and fluency into a single operating rhythm, how to generate momentum predictably, how to partner with leadership, how to plan a 12-month rollout, and how to diagnose acceleration using the SPARK Test. None of this exists earlier in the book. The Activation and Acceleration Guide provides the **sequencing, routines, playbooks, and behavioral guidance** that turn ideas into results. It's the section that ensures the book doesn't just inform; it provides that necessary spark. This is where the reader gains the confidence and clarity to lead, to activate, and to accelerate.

Why Activation Matters

There comes a moment in every catalytic effort when knowing is no longer enough. You've traveled through the frameworks, the canvases, the discipline overviews, and the hard truths about why data work so often stalls. You've recognized your organization in the patterns and barriers we've discussed, and you've seen how Non-Invasive Data Governance, Change Management, and Data Fluency each solve different parts of the puzzle. But insight, on its own, never builds momentum. Recognition doesn't create traction. And enthusiasm rarely survives its first collision with real organizational behavior.

Activation is the moment understanding becomes movement—the spark touching tinder. It's when the ideas in this book shift from being interesting to becoming operational, from "this makes sense" to "this begins now." This section exists for that shift. Not to add more theory, but to help you turn comprehension into acceleration.

Most organizations struggle not because they lack talent or intent, but because they lack a **repeatable way to begin**. They don't know how to structure first steps, pace early wins, or reduce friction without diluting authority. They lack rhythm. Earlier chapters showed how governance clarifies roles and expectations, change management reduces resistance, and fluency builds confidence. Activation is where those three strengths finally operate together: deliberately, predictably, and without overwhelming the business. This is not cheerleading. If excitement alone worked, governance would already be beloved. Activation requires structure, pacing, and the right conditions. It turns the three disciplines from separate initiatives into a single ignition system. What you'll find in this section is a practical, outcome-driven way to spark that system to help your organization feel the shift immediately, not theoretically.

Think back to the introduction of this book and the gut-level reaction many people have to the word *governance*. That reaction isn't just branding—it's history. Governance was too often poorly activated, introduced with rules rather than relevance, and enforced rather than clarified. The Data Catalyst[3] approach gives you a different starting point: alignment, relevance, and proof. Activation is the step that turns those starting points into momentum that the organization can believe in. It is also the moment your role shifts. Up until now, you've been absorbing, comparing, and imagining how these disciplines might work where you are. Activation asks you to step forward as a catalyst-maker— someone who can **start** Non-Invasive Data Governance, who can weave change management into conversations long before resistance appears, and who can create an environment where fluency becomes normal rather than exceptional.

You saw earlier in this book that each discipline contributes something essential: governance clarifies, change prepares, fluency empowers. Activation uses all three to generate energy that compounds over time. Frameworks, canvases, and operating models matter because they give shape to instinct, but activation is what brings them to life. Without it, they are elegant documentation. With it, they become movement.

Activation also matters because transformation requires a **visible beginning**. Quiet improvements are good; catalytic improvements are undeniable. They tell the organization, "this time is different," not because of slogans or ceremonies but because people can actually feel friction decreasing and clarity increasing. Activation produces early evidence using tools like the Data Catalyst³ Spark Alignment Checklist, the Accountability Alignment Matrix, or the Momentum Map, that people can trust. And the need is urgent. Data and AI work is moving faster than most organizations can govern. Tools are appearing faster than risk teams can evaluate them. Fluency gaps are widening. AI behaviors are becoming unpredictable. You don't have time for slow, sequential rollouts. You need ignition; a way to begin confidently without trying to "boil the ocean."

That is why activation is central to The Data Catalyst³ concept. It transforms this model from an appealing idea into a practical advantage. It prevents backsliding into old habits the moment a crisis shows up. And it doesn't require heroics—it requires intentional sequencing, which this guide provides in routines you can apply immediately.

Ultimately, activation matters because it marks your transition. You are no longer someone who understands why governance, change, and fluency matter—you are the person who makes them matter. Someone who can generate movement in places where the organization has historically stalled. Someone who sparks the conditions where people can define, produce, and use data responsibly and confidently.

When you complete this section, you won't simply understand the Data Catalyst³ system; you'll be ready to ignite it. Activation is where traction begins. It's where acceleration becomes possible. And it's the moment your work becomes catalytic.

The Integration Blueprint

If you've read the earlier portions of this book closely, you've already recognized the quiet, costly pattern that shows up in almost every organization: Data Governance, Change Management, and Data Fluency are treated as parallel initiatives rather than coordinated disciplines. They live on separate roadmaps, are led by different leaders, are funded at different levels, are staffed inconsistently, and are communicated unevenly. And the result is exactly what you would expect: governance launches policies without assessing adoption, change teams plan communications without understanding the friction embedded in data quality or definitional ambiguity, and literacy programs teach concepts detached from the messy realities of workflow, tools, and inconsistent data sources. Organizations pay the price in rework, confusion, slow value delivery, and avoidable resistance.

The Integration Blueprint exists to correct this pattern. It is the remedy to fragmentation, and it is the operating system that turns the three disciplines into a single accelerant. Contrary to what people may fear, integration is *not* additional work. It is coordinated work. It is doing the right things at the right times, using the strengths of one discipline to reinforce the others, and creating a rhythm that organizations can follow without overwhelming anyone. Integration is the choreography the business didn't know it needed, and the choreography most leaders have never seen modeled. At its core, the Integration Blueprint is powered by a simple but profound cycle:

Align → Activate → Accelerate

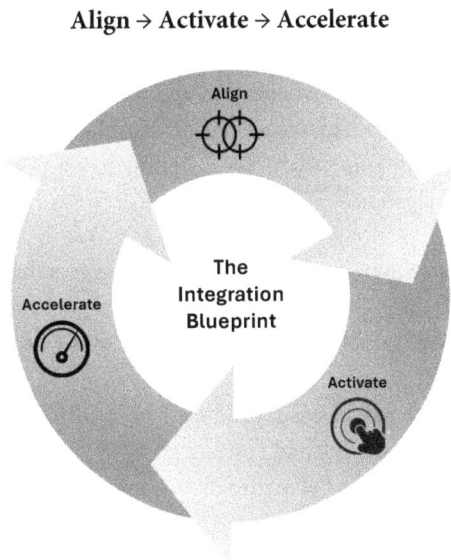

Figure 1: The Integration Blueprint

Those three words form the backbone of everything that follows in this guide. They are the simplest possible articulation of how Data Governance, Change Management, and Data Fluency must interact to produce sustainable momentum. And they represent the flow you will use not only for new initiatives, but also for every AI project, every data improvement effort, every analytics deployment, every policy review, every technology rollout, and every modernization plan in your organization. Let's walk through this cycle with clarity and precision, and most importantly, with repeatability.

ALIGN – Where Clarity Begins

Every data and AI initiative must begin with alignment. Governance takes the lead here because alignment without clarity is just coordinated confusion. This is where to explicitly frame definitions, decisions, ownership, and expectations before work begins. The introduction of Non-Invasive Data Governance explains why clarity is the antidote to chaos, but the Integration Blueprint shows how to put that clarity into motion.

Alignment is not a 3-month planning process or a 200-slide deck. It's a 45-minute alignment routine; a discipline, not a deliverable. You'll use it whenever a project starts, whenever a model is proposed, whenever a workflow changes, or whenever a decision must be made about data that impacts more than one team. The alignment routine asks a short, powerful set of questions:

- What problem are we solving and who cares that it gets solved?
- What decisions will this work require, and who has authority for each?
- What data will be used, produced, or modified, and what is its quality, sensitivity, and readiness?
- What changes to behavior will be required, and where is resistance most likely?
- What fluency gaps must be addressed for people to confidently adopt the output?

Notice how all three disciplines are represented in those questions. Alignment is the moment where governance frames clarity, change predicts human impact, and fluency identifies the readiness gaps. Alignment is the first handoff point in the choreography—and this time, nobody drops the baton.

ACTIVATE – Where Movement Begins

After alignment comes activation, the stage you just explored in the previous paragraphs. But within the Integration Blueprint, activation has a more specific meaning: it is the phase where Change Management takes the lead and moves the project from clarity into motion. Activation is not noise; it is precision. It is where communication begins deliberately, not reactively. It is where roles are prepared intentionally rather than surprised. It is where the people side becomes the enabling force rather than the delaying force.

Here, activation is guided by the monthly triad review; the three-way conversation among governance, change, and fluency leaders that surfaces challenges and keeps the choreography synchronized. The triad review is not a status meeting. It is a momentum check. You evaluate what has moved, where friction has surfaced, and what adjustments are required before friction becomes failure. Within activation, the flow looks like this:

- Governance confirms the clarity of decisions and definitions and ensures alignment is intact.
- Change Management predicts readiness, messaging needs, potential objections, and adoption requirements.
- Data Fluency identifies whether users have the confidence, understanding, and skill to keep pace once the change lands.

Activation turns alignment into traction. In an earlier section, we explored the psychology behind resistance. Here in the Blueprint, you'll learn to operationalize that psychology so resistance never becomes a surprise. Activation ensures that everything launched during alignment has a human path forward.

ACCELERATE – Where Value Compounds

The final step in the sequence is acceleration, where Data Fluency takes the lead. Acceleration is where you guide people not only to adopt the change but to *thrive within it*. It is where competence becomes confidence. It is where teams shift from needing guidance to demonstrating mastery. Acceleration is the proof point of the entire model.

This phase includes the quarterly value checkpoint, where the triad reviews what value has been generated, what stories can be published, and what improvements are needed to sustain momentum. The value checkpoint is not simply a measurement exercise; it is a belief-building exercise. When you publish and celebrate value, you strengthen trust, and trust accelerates everything behind it.

Acceleration also includes the fluency routines, especially the Literacy Tiers and the SPARK alignment pathways. In acceleration, those routines become fully integrated into workflows, onboarding, AI model reviews, and cross-functional decision cycles.

When acceleration is done well:

- Governance becomes normalized rather than negotiated.
- Change becomes anticipated rather than resisted.
- Fluency becomes identity rather than training.

Acceleration completes the cycle, but importantly, it also restarts it. Every acceleration moment triggers a new alignment moment for the next initiative. This loop is the flywheel you will explore in the next part of this section.

How the Blueprint Creates Choreography

To understand the real power of the Integration Blueprint, you must see it as a movement system rather than a compliance mechanism. When the three disciplines interact intentionally, the organization experiences:

1. Fewer surprises
2. Faster adoption
3. Clearer decisions
4. Higher trust
5. More consistent outcomes
6. Reduced rework
7. Greater AI readiness.

The Blueprint prevents the organizational drift that occurs when governance, change, and fluency operate in silos. Instead, it creates choreography:

- Governance brings clarity to Change.
- Change hands readiness to Fluency.
- Fluency hands confidence back to Governance.

This choreography becomes the scaffolding for every initiative moving forward. The Integration Blueprint is not conceptual. It is practical, immediate, and implementable. Here are the rhythms that make it work:

1. The 45-Minute Alignment Routine: Use this whenever a new initiative, model, or workflow starts. It ensures no project moves forward without shared clarity.
2. The Monthly Triad Review: A structured conversation among the leaders of Governance, Change, and Fluency. It keeps friction visible and decisions synchronized.
3. The Quarterly Value Checkpoint: A ritual for publishing wins, analyzing outcomes, and anchoring credibility. This is where you reinforce belief and measure acceleration.
4. The Continuous Rotation: Align → Activate → Accelerate becomes the organizational rhythm. Every initiative moves through it. Every leader begins to expect it. Every team benefits from it.

Why This Blueprint Matters Now

Organizations cannot afford uncoordinated work—not in the age of AI, not in the age of exponential data, not when risk and opportunity are increasing simultaneously. Earlier sections laid the groundwork for why fluency must be raised, showed why change must be shepherded, and proved why governance must be clarified. But *integration* is what allows these disciplines to ignite each other.

The Integration Blueprint is where your work becomes catalytic. It is where you move from frameworks to flow, from understanding to execution, and from scattered effort to synchronized acceleration. When you implement this Blueprint, you don't just manage data, you orchestrate momentum.

In the next section, we deepen this idea by exploring the Momentum Flywheel, the invisible engine that turns choreography into acceleration and acceleration into identity.

The Momentum Flywheel

If the Integration Blueprint provides the choreography, the Momentum Flywheel provides the engine. It is the force multiplier behind everything in this book, the mechanism that transforms a single spark into sustained acceleration. Momentum, when designed intentionally, does more than speed up a project. It reduces friction, builds confidence, amplifies belief, and creates a self-reinforcing cycle where wins come faster and resistance loses its grip. When momentum is present, people move with purpose. When momentum is absent, even simple actions feel like uphill battles. And most organizations, if we're being honest, operate without any real momentum at all.

This part of the Activation and Acceleration Guide exists to change that. The Data Catalyst³ Momentum Flywheel turns momentum from something you hope for into something you engineer. And just like any engine, it has components that interact in a specific sequence, each one powering the next. Four catalytic forces power the Flywheel:

Clarity → Adoption → Fluency → Trust (and back to Clarity)

This is not just a framework; it is the behavioral physics of organizational acceleration. If you revisit The Spark Alignment Canvas and the Non-Invasive Data Governance Operating Model (described in earlier books), you'll see the seeds of this cycle already forming. Clarity reduces confusion. Adoption reduces delays. Fluency reduces errors. Trust reduces resistance. But here, in the Flywheel, these elements become the *motion system* of your transformation.

Let's take each force in turn, then show you how to spin the Flywheel intentionally, how to measure acceleration signals, and how to recover when momentum inevitably stalls.

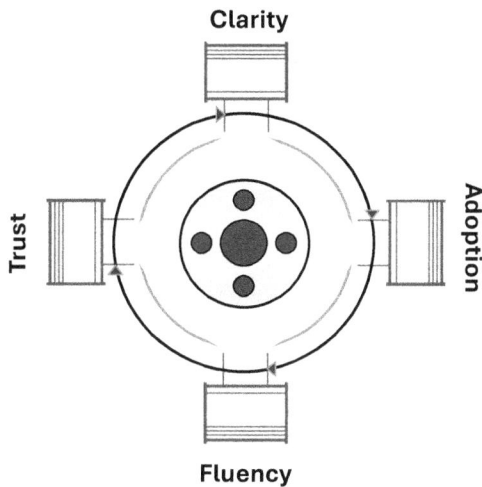

Figure 2: The Momentum Flywheel

Clarity: Momentum's First Push

Momentum begins with clarity because clarity eliminates hesitation. The Flywheel cannot spin until everyone understands what is happening, why it matters, who is accountable, and what decisions must be made. Clarity is the output of Data Governance, specifically Non-Invasive Data Governance (NIDG) at its best. When you establish clarity early, you reduce the number of unknowns that typically slow teams down.

Clarity is not documentation. It is direction:

- **Clarity of purpose**: What outcome are we chasing?
- **Clarity of definitions**: What does this term actually mean?
- **Clarity of authority**: Who decides when to make decisions?
- **Clarity of expectations**: What will change and for whom?

Clarity provides the first lift to the Flywheel by removing the cognitive friction that paralyzes early movement. Without it, everything else drags.

Adoption: Momentum Takes Shape

Once clarity is established, the Flywheel moves into adoption, the domain where Change Management becomes the primary catalyst. Adoption is not the moment people hear about the change; it's the moment people begin acting differently because of the change. Earlier in the book, we focused on why resistance emerges. The Flywheel now focuses on how to convert readiness into movement. Adoption gathers force when:

- People understand the "why" and see themselves in the story.
- Communication is proportional, not performative.
- Leaders reinforce changes visibly, not theoretically.
- Teams experience early wins that prove the change is real.

Adoption is where momentum first becomes visible. Teams begin to move in the same direction. Energy increases. Meetings feel more productive. People stop arguing over definitions and begin making decisions. Adoption creates the forward motion that pulls the Flywheel into its next force.

Fluency: Momentum Stabilizes

Fluency is the phase where confidence catches up to behavior. It is the force that prevents momentum from collapsing under uncertainty. Earlier in the book, we introduced the idea that literacy is not an academic goal; it is an operational requirement. Fluency in this Flywheel is where learning becomes doing. Fluency grows when:

- People have the skills to use the data or AI product effectively.
- Training is practical, role-based, and tied to real workflows.
- Teams feel capable, not intimidated, by new responsibilities.
- Questions are answered quickly and without judgment.

Fluency stabilizes momentum by reducing variability in performance. Without fluency, adoption collapses back into confusion. With fluency, teams build competence that feeds directly into the final force.

Trust: Momentum Amplifies

Trust is the gravitational force of the Flywheel, the one with the greatest pull. When people trust the data, trust the process, trust each other, and trust that governance helps rather than restricts them, everything speeds up. Trust is not a "nice to have." It is the marker of whether the organization is actually accelerating. Trust grows when:

- Wins are visible and validated.
- Data quality improves and stays reliable.
- Decisions made with governed data produce better results.
- Leaders acknowledge and reinforce progress.

Trust is the only force that compounds. One win builds belief in the next. One proof point makes the next proof easier to accept. One cycle of acceleration makes the next cycle faster. Trust is where you start to see exponential returns—the "cubed" part of The Data Catalyst[3] showing up in real organizational behavior.

And this is where the magic happens. Trust loops directly back into clarity. A trusted system makes future alignment easier. People hesitate less. They move faster. They challenge less. They invest more. The Flywheel begins spinning under its own power.

How to Spin the Flywheel Intentionally

Momentum rarely appears by accident. It emerges through deliberate, predictable actions. Here is the playbook for spinning the Flywheel on purpose:

1. **Start with a Clarity Burst**: Use the 45-minute alignment routine to set direction. This creates the initial force required to move the Flywheel.
2. **Launch a Quick, Visible Adoption Win**: Use a ≤60-day quick win to demonstrate early traction. The goal isn't perfection; it's proof.
3. **Build Fluency in the Moments That Matter**: Identify the 2–3 behaviors that matter most and provide precisely the literacy needed to support them. No more, no less.
4. **Publish Trust Signals Relentlessly**: Share evidence, screenshots, improved metrics, user testimonials—anything that strengthens belief.
5. **Repeat the Cycle Without Waiting**: Do not wait for the next initiative. Apply the Flywheel to everyday decisions, meetings, and reviews. The more frequently you restart it, the faster it turns.

Acceleration Signals: How You Know the Flywheel Is Working

When momentum begins to take hold, you will see it before you feel it. Look for these signals:

- Meetings shorten because clarity increases.
- Teams escalate fewer issues because ownership is understood.
- People ask higher-quality questions because fluency rises.
- Projects move faster without heroics because trust stabilizes behavior.
- Value becomes easier to publish because evidence accumulates.

These signals appear subtly at first. But the more they accumulate, the more undeniable the acceleration becomes.

The Seven Momentum Killers (and How to Neutralize Them)

Momentum is fragile, especially early. These seven killers appear in almost every organization:

1. **Ambiguous Ownership**: When no one knows who decides, everything slows. **Solution**: Use the Accountability Alignment Matrix every time.
2. **Overcommunication Without Meaning**: Noise kills adoption. **Solution**: Use concise, audience-specific reframes.
3. **Training Without Context**: Fluency collapses when learning is abstract. **Solution**: Tie every lesson to a real workflow.
4. **Governance as Gatekeeping**: Control slows momentum. **Solution**: Apply NIDG. Embed governance into existing processes rather than adding gates.
5. **Tool Fixation**: Tools amplify momentum but cannot generate it. **Solution**: Focus on behaviors first, tools second.
6. **Lack of Evidence**: Without visible wins, trust cannot grow. **Solution**: Publish quick proofs early and often.
7. **Leadership Drift**: Momentum decays when leaders stop modeling belief. **Solution**: Reinforce leadership commitments.

Neutralize these killers early and momentum becomes much easier to preserve.

Why the Flywheel Is the Heart of Acceleration

Momentum is not optional anymore. In the AI era, organizations that move slowly will not simply lag—they will lose. The Data Catalyst[3] is a system built for acceleration, and the Momentum Flywheel is where acceleration becomes measurable, visible, and repeatable. It shifts your organization from episodic improvement to continuous improvement, from isolated wins to compounding wins, from temporary success to sustained advantage.

When the Flywheel is spinning, everything else in the book becomes easier: governance feels natural, change feels expected, literacy feels useful, and AI feels safer. The Flywheel is where the transformation becomes the culture.

The Leadership Accord

If the Momentum Flywheel explains *how* acceleration happens, the Leadership Accord explains *who* must make acceleration possible and what they must consistently do to sustain it. No catalytic effort succeeds without leadership, but the kind of leadership required in today's environment is very different from what most organizations are accustomed to. Governance once lived quietly in back rooms. Change management surfaced occasionally around large transformations. Data literacy was often treated as optional professional development. But the convergence of data, risk, and AI has changed that landscape permanently. Leaders now operate in a world where decisions carry exponential consequences: ethical, operational, reputational, and financial. And those consequences show up faster than ever before.

In this world, "executive sponsorship" is insufficient. It is foundational, but it is not a differentiator. Executives who merely sponsor governance will see slow compliance. Executives who *actively shape the conditions in which governance, change, and fluency can thrive* will see acceleration. The Leadership Accord exists to codify that shift. It clarifies the commitments required from executives and the reciprocal commitments required from data teams. The Accord is not a contract; it is a shared leadership practice that governs the relationship between authority and accountability, direction and execution, acceleration and risk management. It is the connective tissue that ensures the entire Data Catalyst³ concept becomes not just operational, but cultural.

Why a Leadership Accord Matters Now

Throughout earlier sections of this book, we have shown how the three catalysts, Data Governance, Change Management, and Data Fluency, must be integrated to function as a single accelerant. But integration cannot happen solely within the data team. It must be modeled, reinforced, and protected by leadership. Organizations that lack a Leadership Accord typically show one of three patterns:

1. Governance becomes overpowered by political turbulence, losing momentum every time leadership changes or priorities shift.
2. Change work becomes performative, reduced to communication blasts rather than meaningful behavior change.
3. Literacy becomes a "nice to have", delivered as training sessions that do not influence decisions, models, or mission outcomes.

The Leadership Accord solves these failures by articulating expectations on both sides. Executives create the conditions and data teams deliver the proof. Executives set the tone and data teams sustain the cadence. Executives reinforce priorities and data teams reinforce trust.

This partnership reflects the very heart of Non-Invasive Data Governance, where governance is not a policing function but a shared accountability model embedded into everyday work. Section Eight is where all of these threads come together, and the Leadership Accord ensures they remain strong under real-world pressure.

Executive Commitments	Data Team Commitments
Champion Governed Decisions Publicly	**Deliver Early Proof**
Executives model governed behavior by using trusted data, validated definitions, and lineage-backed insights in visible forums. This normalizes clarity and signals that governed decision-making is the organizational standard.	Data teams provide rapid, visible evidence of progress, especially within the first 60 days. Proof builds trust and accelerates momentum, reinforcing the principles of the Momentum Flywheel.
Shield Governance From Turbulence	**Remain Non-Invasive by Design**
Leadership protects governance efforts from shifting priorities, reorganizations, or crisis-driven distractions. Continuity ensures that governance becomes a backbone, not a casualty, of organizational change.	Data teams embed governance into existing workflows rather than creating new gates. This reduces resistance, improves adoption, and operationalizes the principles of Non-Invasive Data Governance introduced earlier in the book.
Enforce Accountability Consistently	**Prioritize Relevance Over Complexity**
Executives expect definitions, decisions, and quality thresholds to be followed once approved. Enforcement builds organizational alignment and prevents governance from becoming merely advisory.	Data teams simplify governance concepts, translate technical language into business terms, and anchor all recommendations to mission or business outcomes. Complexity slows the Flywheel; relevance accelerates it.
Elevate Literacy as a Strategic Priority	**Embed Governance Into Daily Workflow**
Leaders treat fluency as a core capability required for AI readiness, operational confidence, and risk reduction. Fluency growth accelerates when leaders frame it as essential to performance and not optional.	Teams move governance upstream into intake, design, development, and review cycles so quality, consistency, and accountability are built in rather than inspected later. Governance becomes part of the work, not an afterthought.
Celebrate and Scale Early Wins	**Treat Literacy as an Ongoing Relationship**
Executives amplify small wins to reinforce belief, demonstrate progress, and energize momentum. This boosts the trust component of the Flywheel and inspires cross-functional adoption.	Data teams reinforce literacy concepts over time, refresh examples as tools and data evolve, and partner with business leaders to turn literacy into a continuous capability rather than one-off instruction.

Table 10: The Leadership Accord

Executive Commitments: What Leadership Must Bring

The first half of the Accord outlines what executives commit to—not aspiration-ally, but behavior-ally. These commitments are not ceremonial; they are operational. Each one directly fuels the Flywheel.

1. **Champion Governed Decisions Publicly**: Executives must model governed behavior in the open. When the CEO, CDAO, or CIO uses governed definitions, references trusted metrics, or insists on lineage validation, the organization follows. This is how clarity (the first force of the Flywheel) becomes cultural rather than episodic.

2. **Shield Governance From Turbulence**: Organizations shift priorities constantly, but governance cannot be allowed to reset every six months. Executives must provide continuity, especially during organizational changes, leadership transitions, or emerging crises. Shielding governance does not mean slowing change; it means preserving the structures that allow change to succeed.

3. **Enforce Accountability With Consistency**: Leaders must expect teams to follow decisions, definitions, and quality thresholds once they are agreed upon. Accountability is not punishment; it is alignment. This commitment ensures that governance does not become advisory; it becomes operational.

4. **Elevate Literacy to Strategic Priority**: Executives must treat data fluency not as training, but as a critical capability. When leaders talk about literacy as essential to risk reduction, mission readiness, and AI confidence, fluency grows faster and farther. The Literacy tiers earlier in the book become truly actionable only when prioritized at the top.

5. **Celebrate and Scale Early Wins**: Momentum stalls when leadership ignores progress. Executives must amplify the 60-day quick wins established earlier in the book and use those wins to build belief and trust across departments.

These commitments define the leadership environment in which acceleration becomes possible. Without them, even the best-designed governance systems will stall.

Data Team Commitments: What Practitioners Bring

Partnership requires reciprocity. The second half of the Accord defines what data teams commit to, not in theory, but in practice:

1. **Deliver Early Proof**: The Data Catalyst³ model relies on rapid, visible wins. Data teams must commit to delivering evidence early and often. This is how organizations build trust in the data, which, as we saw earlier in this section, is the final force of the Momentum Flywheel.

2. **Remain Non-Invasive by Design**: NIDG is a core principle of this book. Data teams must commit to embedding governance into existing processes, not adding bureaucracy. This accelerates adoption and reduces resistance during early phases of activation.

3. **Prioritize Relevance Over Complexity**: Data teams must translate governance, change, and literacy into language and actions the business understands. Complexity slows the Flywheel; relevance accelerates it.

4. **Embed Governance Into Workflow, Not Afterthoughts**: Governance must not sit at the end of the process, acting as a gate. Data teams commit to bringing governance upstream into intake, design, model development, testing, and production.

5. **Treat Literacy as an Ongoing Relationship**: Fluency cannot be a one-off training event. Data teams commit to partnering with business leaders to reinforce concepts, share new examples, and expand capability in cycles rather than one-time sessions.

These commitments ensure that data teams are not waiting for leadership to act, they are activating in tandem.

How the Accord Accelerates Everything Else

The accord turns three separate disciplines into a single leadership system. Instead of leadership saying, "govern better," leadership says:

- "We will reinforce governed decisions."
- "We will remove barriers for you."
- "We will amplify your wins."
- "We will model the behaviors we expect."

And the data team responds:

- "We will prove value early."
- "We will keep governance non-invasive."
- "We will embed governance into work, not add work."
- "We will build capability, not confusion."

This mutual clarity, this shared operating compact, reinforces every section of the book. It strengthens alignment, clarifies ownership, accelerates people-side adoption, and sustains learning. It is the connective architecture behind the entire Data Catalyst³ model.

With the Leadership Accord in place, the organization doesn't just implement Data Governance, Change Management, and Data Fluency; it accelerates them.

The 12-Month Roadmap

Now the question becomes: *How do I bring all of this to life in my organization without overwhelming everyone, including myself?*

This is where the 12-Month Catalyst Roadmap enters. It is not a project plan. It is not a checklist, a maturity model, or a transformation mandate. It is a sequence (a rhythm) designed to help you build momentum in a world where business demands, budget cycles, leadership priorities, and technological pressures change constantly. It is a way of introducing The Data Catalyst³ approach into your ecosystem in a manner that is paced, grounded, and deeply non-invasive.

Ideas do not transform organizations. Rhythms do. Rhythms create expectation. Expectation creates habit. Habit creates identity. The 12-Month Catalyst Roadmap is built on those principles. It gives you four discipline-aligned phases: **Foundation** → **Activation** → **Expansion** → **Acceleration**. Each lasts roughly one quarter, though the timing can flex without breaking the model. The goal is not to create more work. The goal is to guide the organization toward doing the right work at the right time.

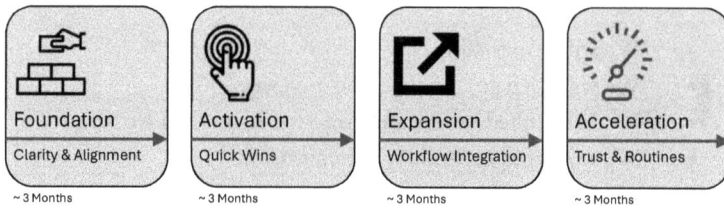

Foundation	Activation	Expansion	Acceleration
Clarity & Alignment	Quick Wins	Workflow Integration	Trust & Routines
~ 3 Months	~ 3 Months	~ 3 Months	~ 3 Months

Figure 3: The Catalyst Roadmap

This roadmap is the bridge between knowing and becoming. And in the age of AI, where governance failures are amplified, change saturation is constant, and fluency gaps directly impact risk—there has never been a more necessary time to become.

Phase 1: Foundation (Months 1–3)

Purpose: Establish clarity, credibility, and alignment: the elements that power the first turn of the Momentum Flywheel.

The Foundation phase is the moment when you set the stage for every catalytic action that follows. Just like building a house requires more attention to leveling the ground than installing the roof, building a Catalyst organization requires you to set structural clarity before you take on transformative workloads.

In the Foundation phase, you are not "implementing governance." You are not selling change. You are not teaching literacy at scale. You are establishing the *conditions under which the catalysts can operate together.* This phase is intentionally light in workload but heavy in alignment.

1. **Establish True North:** Your True North is the concrete expression of why governance, change, and fluency matter in

your context. It must tie directly to business value, mission impact, or risk reduction. Without it, every decision becomes negotiable; with it, decisions become anchored. In the Foundation phase, you finalize True North with your executive sponsor, ideally the person who will sign the Leadership Accord.

2. **Launch the Glossary:** You begin with the 10–20 high-value terms collected across business areas. This is not the "enterprise glossary" that eats six months and three committees. This is a governance accelerant: a shared language that reduces friction immediately. In the Foundation phase, it is small, but the impact is huge: alignment, clarity, and reduced noise.

3. **Form the Catalyst Triad:** As you saw earlier in the book, the Catalyst Triad is the operational leadership structure consisting of governance, change, and fluency. These do not need to be three separate people; in many organizations, they are roles and not titles. The Triad becomes your month-over-month engine. In this phase, you simply identify the roles, define expectations, and set meeting rhythms.

4. **Apply the Data Catalyst³ Spark Alignment Checklist:** The Data Catalyst³ Spark Alignment Checklist becomes your first real instrument. In the Foundation phase, you use it to shape the scope and expectations for the first quick-win initiative. Strategy, Participation, Adoption, Reinforcement, Knowledge transfer, all five SPARK dimensions begin to surface.

Deliverables for Phase 1
- Completed True North statement.
- Initial (lightweight) Glossary v1.
- Defined Catalyst Triad roles plus 60-minute monthly meetings scheduled.
- First Data Catalyst³ Spark Alignment Checklist drafted for your selected initiative.

Checkpoints
- Do leaders understand why the Catalyst approach matters?

- Does the business understand, at least at a high level, what's coming?
- Are you identifying quick wins rather than large transformations?

Red Flags
- Trying to scale literacy too early.
- Attempting enterprise-wide policy changes before clarity is established.
- No executive time invested in True North.
- A triad in name only, not in practice.

Phase 2: Activation (Months 4–6)

Purpose: Move from clarity to action. Give people what they need to begin, not what they need to finish.

Activation is where the spark hits the tinder. In this phase, you begin using the instruments introduced in earlier sections as true accelerants, and not artifacts. You are not building a governance program; you are building governed behavior. You are not launching a change "plan"; you are enabling adoption. You are not creating literacy materials; you are building capability that directly supports the first quick-win initiative.

1. **Implement the Accountability Alignment Matrix:** This is where governance becomes visible. By clarifying Responsible, Accountable, Consulted, and Informed roles, as well as Decision Authority, you remove ambiguity. Governance becomes structural, not sentimental. The matrix is applied specifically to the initiative identified in the Data Catalyst³ Spark Alignment Checklist. Start small. Impact big.
2. **Define the Change Pathway:** The Change Pathway identifies who must change what, by when, and with what support. It is lightweight and intensely practical. In Activation, you customize it to the initiative you selected in Phase 1. It reframes change from messaging into behavior.

3. **Launch the First Quick-Win Cycle (60-Day Win):** Earlier in the book, we defined the importance of delivering evidence in ≤60 days. Your first quick win happens here. It should be small enough to complete fast but meaningful enough to publish: a reduction in reporting conflicts, a resolved definition dispute, a trusted score rebuilt for analytics, or a model review completed using governance criteria.

Deliverables for Phase 2
- Accountability Alignment Matrix defined for your initiative.
- Change Pathway developed for impacted roles.
- First 60-day quick-win delivered.
- Before/after evidence captured.

Checkpoints
- Is the triad meeting monthly and adjusting roles?
- Are people beginning to recognize governed decisions as "the way we work"?
- Are managers supporting and not resisting behavior changes?

Red Flags

- Trying to turn the quick win into a large project.
- Delivering "outputs" but not "evidence".
- Governance drifting toward enforcement instead of acceleration.
- Change management treated as communication rather than a shift in behavior.

Phase 3: Expansion (Months 7–9)

Purpose: Expand capability without expanding burden. Spread value and not bureaucracy.

This is the moment when the organization begins to feel the shift. The first quick win has created belief. The glossary is growing naturally. The Triad is meeting predictably. The Accountability Alignment Matrix is reducing friction. And now you extend this capability across more areas, without burdening the business or the triad with unnecessary complexity:

1. **Embed Governance into Workflow:** Instead of introducing governance at the end of a project (as a review or checkpoint), you embed it into intake, scoping, quality rules, model development, and system enhancements. This is Non-Invasive Data Governance in action. People follow governance because it is the simplest way to do their job, and not an extra step.

2. **Scale Practical Literacy:** You introduce the Literacy Tiers of Foundational, Functional, and Applied, and how they align to roles. You are not creating a university program; you are building fluency that supports decision-making. In this phase, literacy becomes relevant, contextual, and tied to real work rather than an academic exercise.

3. **Establish Cross-Functional Decision Routines:** With multiple teams now participating, decisions must become smoother, faster, and more transparent. You implement lightweight routines such as 20-minute decision triages, weekly domain-owner syncs, and quarterly decision reviews. These routines eliminate ambiguity and accelerate adoption.

Deliverables for Phase 3
- Governance embedded in selected workflows.
- Literacy Tiers launched (with examples tailored to your business).
- Cross-functional decision routines are operational.
- Two additional quick wins delivered.

Checkpoints
- Are people using the glossary because it works and not because they were told to?
- Is the volume of data disputes decreasing?
- Are teams using the Accountability Alignment Matrix without prompting?

Red Flags
- Literacy being pushed as training rather than a capability.
- "Governance creep," where teams attempt to over-engineer.
- Decision routines turning into bureaucratic meetings.

Phase 4: Acceleration (Months 10–12)

Purpose: Make acceleration the default state, and not a novelty.

Acceleration is not about going faster. It is about going faster *with clarity, trust, and alignment*. It is the phase where the Catalyst identity takes root, where the principles of The Data Catalyst[3] become self-reinforcing, and where the triad becomes a true strategic partner to leadership:

1. **Measure Trust:** Trust becomes quantifiable. You use trust scoring, whether through surveys, operational indicators, or quality metrics, to assess how the organization perceives data, decisions, and definitions. Trust is not a feeling; it is a signal. And in this phase, signals matter.
2. **Publish Stories and Proof:** Governance wins are often quiet. Change wins are often invisible. Literacy wins are often personal. Publishing stories makes them cultural. You highlight before/after evidence, showcase domain owners, spotlight analysts who solved real problems, and celebrate teams who prevented AI risks. These stories create belief and belief accelerates everything.
3. **Reinforce Value Routines:** You begin establishing rituals: quarterly Catalyst Reviews, annual Fluency Refreshes, semiannual Accountability reviews, and monthly governance huddles. These routines make the Catalyst system predictable, durable, and scalable.
4. **Transition Catalyst Practices Into Organizational Habit:** Acceleration becomes culture when it becomes memory. You embed Catalyst practices into onboarding, role expectations, performance conversations, and model governance procedures. You are no longer "implementing governance"; you are institutionalizing clarity, adoption, fluency, and trust.

Deliverables for Phase 4
- Trust scoring implemented and baseline measured.
- Three published stories and one executive showcase.
- Catalyst routines institutionalized.
- Catalyst practices embedded into at least one enterprise process.

Checkpoints
- Are teams asking for Catalyst support rather than avoiding it?
- Are literacy gaps shrinking?
- Are data disputes resolving faster?
- Is leadership reinforcing governed decisions publicly?

Red Flags
- Momentum slowing due to leadership distraction.
- Routines that devolve into reporting instead of learning.
- New leaders pulling governance back into IT-only territory.

Why This Roadmap Works

The 12-Month Catalyst Roadmap works because it is grounded in human behavior, organizational reality, and the accelerant nature of the three catalysts. It is not a top-heavy, policy-first approach. It is a movement-first approach: governed, supported, and skill-enabled. It works because:

- It follows the natural sequence of how organizations learn.
- It creates early value that builds belief.
- It respects change saturation.
- It ties governance to real work immediately.
- It prevents literacy from becoming theory.
- It distributes responsibility without diluting accountability.
- It makes acceleration measurable.

Most importantly, it replaces overwhelm with order.

The SPARK Test

By now, you've absorbed a tremendous amount of content: disciplines, canvases, examples, stories, and a roadmap for the first year of transformation. But before we move to the final parts of this guide, we need to address a question that plagues nearly every data, AI, governance, or transformation initiative I've ever encountered:

> *How do you know whether any of this is actually working?*

Organizations love the illusion of progress. They love maturity models, dashboards, RAG (retrieve, augment, generate) status markers, and quarterly updates that make it sound like everything is marching forward. But in reality, many of those indicators measure activity rather than acceleration. They measure volume, and not behavior. They measure how much is being produced, and not how much is being adopted. In a catalytic system, none of that is enough.

If The Data Catalyst[3] is about anything, it is about changing how the organization moves, including how it makes decisions, adopts new practices, reduces friction, builds trust, and ultimately turns intention into acceleration. Those outcomes cannot be measured by counting artifacts. They must be measured by observing behavior.

That is the purpose of the SPARK Test.

Unlike a maturity model, which encourages organizations to climb theoretical ladders, the SPARK Test asks a simpler but far more consequential set of questions: *Are you accelerating? Are the catalysts taking root? Are people behaving differently today than they were yesterday?* If the answer is "yes," you are on your way. If the answer is "no," the SPARK Test tells you exactly where to intervene.

This is not a one-time assessment. It is a living instrument that evolves as your organization evolves. It becomes your early warning system, your alignment compass, your confidence gauge, and your behavior barometer.

SPARK stands for Strategy, Participation, Adoption, Reinforcement, and Knowledge Transfer: the five behaviors that determine whether catalytic work will take hold. Let's take them one at a time.

Strategy: Are We Aligned to Outcomes?

Strategy is the first dimension because it is the foundation of everything else in The Data Catalyst³. You saw this earlier when we explored True North, and you saw it reinforced across the canvases and the 12-Month Roadmap. Without strategic alignment, governance becomes episodic, change becomes cosmetic, and literacy becomes academic. Strategy is the anchor that prevents drift. The Strategy dimension of the SPARK Test asks three simple behavioral questions:

1. Do teams consistently reference True North when making decisions?
2. Are data, AI, and governance initiatives directly tied to measurable outcomes? Not vague aspirations but concrete outcomes.
3. Is there visible consistency in priorities across business, technical, and leadership groups?

You score Strategy on a scale from 0 to 5, and not based on how many strategic documents exist, but on how strategic behavior shows up in meetings, decisions, trade-offs, and escalations.

- 0–1: Strategy is aspirational but disconnected from work.
- 2–3: Strategy is understood but inconsistently applied.
- 4–5: Strategy guides decisions daily and reduces friction because everyone knows what matters most.

Common warning signs include leaders approving work that contradicts True North, teams asking "why are we doing this?" weeks into a project, or domain squabbles over priorities. Improvement pathways include revisiting True North with leadership, linking artifacts to outcomes in the Data Catalyst[3] Spark Alignment Checklist, or publicly reinforcing strategic alignment in leadership forums.

> *Strategy is not about having a plan.*
> *It is about making decisions that honor it.*

Participation: Right People Engaged in the Right Ways?

Participation isn't attendance. It isn't meeting volume. It isn't how many people show up to a workshop. Participation is about preparedness, responsibility, and contribution. It is about the quality of engagement, not the quantity. This dimension reinforces the core principle of Non-Invasive Data Governance: that governance works when people engage through their existing role-based responsibilities, and not as an extra job.

The SPARK Test evaluates participation by examining:

1. **Role clarity**: Do people know where they fit in governance, change, and literacy?
2. **Preparedness**: Do participants come to decisions with data, analysis, and context ready? Not opinions but evidence.
3. **Ownership**: When friction arises, do people escalate wisely and resolve issues quickly, rather than defer them?

A score of 0–1 suggests you have positional governance—titles without participation. A score of 4–5 indicates distributed stewardship is working: the organization is rowing in the same direction without being told to.

Warning signs include passive silence during reviews, recurring escalations caused by the same individuals, or domain owners who are "owners" only on paper. Improvement pathways include tightening R/A/C/I ownership, using the triad to coach roles, or embedding participation expectations into routine governance check-ins.

> *Participation is the oxygen of catalytic work.*
> *Without it, nothing ignites.*

Adoption: Are People Using the New Ways of Working?

This is one of the most essential dimensions because it tells you whether change is operational rather than theatrical. Adoption is observable behavior: what people do, not what they say. The SPARK Test evaluates adoption by looking at:

1. Use of governed definitions, data assets, and workflows.
2. Has the glossary replaced hallway definitions? Are people using certified data sources instead of side spreadsheets?
3. Model behavior: Are teams using governance criteria in AI and analytics work?
4. Decision hygiene: Are decisions traced to trusted data? Are disputes resolved faster?

Adoption is scored by watching behavior, and not surveying opinion:

- 0–1: Teams acknowledge the rules but circumvent them.
- 2–3: Teams use the new practices inconsistently.
- 4–5: Teams use governed practices because they are easier, and not because they're mandated.

Warning signs include back-channel spreadsheets resurfacing, repeated mis-definitions, or "crypto-governance", where teams build their own definitions outside the system. Improvement pathways include embedding governance earlier in the workflow, increasing transparency in decision-making, or simplifying governed processes to make them the path of least resistance.

> *Adoption is the heartbeat of momentum.*
> *Without it, everything else stalls.*

Reinforcement: Are We Making New Behaviors Stick?

Reinforcement is where catalytic work becomes culture. Change does not persist because you communicated it well. It persists because it is reinforced rhythmically, consistently, and non-invasively. The Reinforcement dimension of the SPARK Test observes:

1. Repetition of routines: Are governance routines, triad syncs, literacy refreshes, and decision rituals happening predictably?
2. Visibility: Are wins, stories, and value signals being published? Is leadership reinforcing governed decisions publicly?
3. Integration: Are Catalyst practices being pulled into onboarding, KPIs, model reviews, project intake, and quarterly planning?

A score of 0–1 signals episodic reinforcement, in which practices appear only during crises or leadership campaigns. A score of 4–5 reflects cultural reinforcement, where Catalyst practices are a natural part of how the organization operates.

Warning signs include missed routines, leadership drift, a collapse in storytelling, or over-reliance on one champion. Improvement pathways include reinstating quarterly Catalyst Reviews, bringing value stories back into leadership updates, or tying reinforcement into performance and planning cycles.

> *Reinforcement is the bridge from acceleration to identity.*
> *Without it, momentum evaporates.*

Knowledge Transfer: Are We Growing Facility, Not Just Knowledge?

This is the most underestimated dimension of transformation, and one of the most essential in the age of AI. Knowledge Transfer evaluates whether literacy is translating into improved decisions, reduced risk, and better outcomes. Knowledge Transfer is not training. It is comprehension in action. The SPARK Test evaluates it through:

1. **Role-based fluency**: Do people understand the data concepts necessary for *their* decisions?
2. **Confidence**: Are individuals confident using governed data, AI-supported outputs, or literacy-enhanced insights?
3. **Capability**: Do decisions made with greater fluency result in fewer errors, fewer rework cycles, or reduced risk?

A score of 0–1 suggests literacy is episodic: attended, forgotten, unadopted. A score of 4–5 suggests literacy is embedded: practical, contextual, and catalytic.

Warning signs include confused requests for data, overreliance on a small set of experts, inconsistent use of AI tools, or repeated misunderstandings of definitions. Improvement pathways include expanding literacy tiers, connecting literacy to real workflows, or using "learning sprints" tied to actual projects.

Knowledge Transfer is where fluency becomes fuel.
Without it, governance and change slow to a crawl.

Putting SPARK Together: Your Behavior Scorecard

When you combine the five dimensions of Strategy, Participation, Adoption, Reinforcement, and Knowledge Transfer, you create a behavior-based picture of your organization's catalytic health.

A low SPARK score does not indicate failure. It indicates opportunity. A high SPARK score does not indicate completion. It indicates momentum.

The SPARK Test is designed to be used quarterly. That cadence aligns with the rhythms established in the 12-Month Roadmap, reinforces the triad's responsibilities, and connects directly to the stories and routines outlined in earlier sections. When used consistently, the SPARK Test becomes:

- A lead indicator of success rather than a lagging indicator of failure.
- A conversation starter between leadership and data teams.
- A diagnostic tool for pinpointing bottlenecks before they become crises.
- A behavioral compass for organizational alignment.
- A proof instrument for demonstrating real acceleration.

S – Strategy	P – Participation	A – Adoption	R – Reinforcement	K – Knowledge Transfer
Are we aligned to outcomes?	Are the right people engaged?	Are people using the new ways of working?	Are we reinforcing new behaviors so they stick?	Are we growing capability, not just knowledge?
Behavioral Questions • Do teams reference True North when making decisions? • Are initiatives tied to measurable outcomes, not aspirations? • Are priorities consistent across leadership, business, and technical groups?	**Behavioral Questions** • Do people understand their role-based responsibilities? • Do participants come prepared with evidence? • Do domain owners escalate wisely and resolve friction quickly?	**Behavioral Questions** • Are governed definitions and certified sources consistently used? • Are side spreadsheets disappearing? • Are governance criteria used in analytics and AI work? • Are decisions being traced to trusted data?	**Behavioral Questions** • Are governance routines, triad syncs, and decision rituals happening predictably? • Are wins, stories, and evidence being published consistently? • Are Catalyst practices embedded into onboarding, KPIs, intake, and planning cycles?	**Behavioral Questions** • Do people understand the data/AI concepts needed for their role? • Are individuals confident interpreting governed data or AI outputs? • Do decisions show fewer errors, rework cycles, or risk exposure?
Scoring (0–5) • 0–1: Strategy disconnected from work. • 2–3: Strategy understood but inconsistently applied. • 4–5: Strategy visibly drives daily decisions.	**Scoring (0–5)** • 0–1: Participation positional, not behavioral. • 2–3: Uneven engagement across teams. • 4–5: Distributed stewardship functioning effectively.	**Scoring (0–5)** • 0–1: Teams circumvent governance. • 2–3: Mixed adoption across roles. • 4–5: Governed behavior is the path of least resistance.	**Scoring (0–5)** • 0–1: Reinforcement is episodic and crisis-driven. • 2–3: Some routines exist but lack consistency. • 4–5: Reinforcement is rhythmic, cultural, and self-sustaining.	**Scoring (0–5)** • 0–1: Literacy is episodic—attended, forgotten, unused. • 2–3: Knowledge exists but doesn't influence behavior. • 4–5: Fluency is contextual, applied, and improves outcomes.
Warning Signs • Priorities conflict between teams. • Work approved that contradicts True North. • Teams ask, "Why are we doing this?" mid-project.	**Warning Signs** • Silent or unprepared meetings. • Repeated escalations from same individuals. • Ownership unclear or ignored.	**Warning Signs** • Back-channel sources reappear. • Definitions inconsistent across teams. • "Crypto-governance" develops in pockets.	**Warning Signs** • Missed or irregular governance routines. • Leadership stops reinforcing governed decisions publicly. • Storytelling and value visibility disappear. • Reliance on one champion instead of distributed reinforcement.	**Warning Signs** • Confusing data requests or repeated misunderstandings. • Over-dependence on a small set of experts. • Misuse or misinterpretation of AI tools. • Persistent definition or lineage misunderstandings.
Improvement Paths • Re-align True North with leadership. • Tie all artifacts to outcomes in the SPARK Canvas. • Reinforce strategy in executive communications.	**Improvement Paths** • Strengthen R/A/C/I clarity. • Use triad coaching to recalibrate roles. • Embed expectations into governance routines.	**Improvement Paths** • Move governance further upstream. • Increase transparency in decision-making. • Simplify governed workflows to encourage adoption.	**Improvement Paths** • Re-establish quarterly Catalyst Reviews. • Add value stories to regular leadership updates. • Tie governance behaviors to performance and planning cycles. • Rebuild predictable routines (monthly triad, decision huddles, literacy refreshes).	**Improvement Paths** • Expand Literacy Tiers aligned to roles. • Tie literacy sessions to real workflows and current initiatives. • Use learning sprints connected to actual projects. • Reinforce fluency in model reviews, design sessions, and post-mortems.

Table 11: The SPARK Test

SPARK becomes your internal accelerant audit, a way to ensure that the catalysts you are building are actually producing catalytic movement.

A Living Instrument for a Moving Organization

No organization ever stands still, especially in the age of AI, regulatory uncertainty, rapid digitization, and overlapping initiatives. Tools that depend on static assessments or ceremonial scoring fall apart under real-world pressures. That is why the SPARK Test is intentionally simple, behavioral, and repeatable. It evolves with your organization. It grows alongside your Catalyst maturity. And it becomes more valuable as more teams participate.

The beauty of SPARK is that it never asks you to model perfection. It only asks you to observe reality.

- Are we aligned?
- Are we engaged?
- Are we adopting?
- Are we reinforcing?
- Are we transferring knowledge?

If the answer to most of these is "yes," your organization is accelerating. If the answer is "sometimes," you have clarity on where to focus. If the answer is "not yet," then SPARK becomes the ignition point, and not the indictment.

In a world where organizations struggle to measure momentum, SPARK gives you something better: a way to measure the behaviors that create it.

Using the Disciplines Together

Across this book, we explored Data Governance, Change Management, and Data Fluency as distinct disciplines, each with its own purpose, strengths, and natural points of influence. But in practice, these disciplines were never meant to operate alone. Their real catalytic force emerges only when they function as a single, coordinated system. When organizations treat governance, change, and fluency as separate initiatives, they unknowingly create drag. Governance introduces clarity but lacks adoption. Change generates momentum but ignores data friction. Literacy builds awareness but fails to connect to real work. When woven together, however, these three disciplines eliminate uncertainty, reduce resistance, and set the conditions for data and AI work to move faster with far fewer surprises. Together, they become the accelerant that organizations have been missing.

The secret is not to combine the disciplines into one monolithic program or to assign a single team to "own" all three. The power comes from rotation: using governance, change, and fluency at the moments where each is most valuable. This rotational approach is consistent with non-invasive principles. When you deliberately rotate disciplines, you avoid overwhelming teams with process and instead give them exactly what they need at exactly the right time. Governance sets the rules of clarity and accountability, change management prepares and supports people as behaviors shift, and fluency provides the practical comprehension needed to make good decisions. None of these disciplines can compensate for the absence of the others. Together, they create the environment where the spark of acceleration becomes sustainable energy.

This guide explains how to apply that rotation across every project, initiative, and model lifecycle. It begins with project onboarding: the point where most organizations unintentionally bake in confusion. When a project is first proposed, governance should be the first discipline to engage. Not to slow the project down, but to create the clarity that prevents downstream rework. This is where the Data Catalyst[3] Spark Alignment Checklist provides immediate value: identifying intended outcomes, clarifying which data domains are involved, naming accountable stewards, and surfacing trust risks before they become political battles. Once governance has established clarity, the rotation moves to change management, which ensures stakeholders understand the impacts, expectations, and behavior shifts required for the work ahead. Only after these two steps does fluency come into play, ensuring that every participant understands the concepts, terminology, and decision points that matter most for that specific initiative. The order matters. Governance creates direction, change builds commitment, and fluency equips people to act with confidence.

Beyond onboarding, the rotation becomes even more powerful during cross-functional planning. This is where governance ensures decisions are made with the right data, by the right people, with the right authority. You can trace the benefits of this approach directly to the Accountability Alignment Matrix. By establishing clarity across teams, governance prevents the gridlock and disagreement that so often stall progress. With that clarity in place, change management creates alignment and prepares each team for the collaboration required, reducing friction, managing expectations, and resolving competing priorities before they derail momentum. Fluency then enhances the planning process by ensuring teams understand the data concepts that underpin their work, enabling them to interact effectively and avoid misinterpretations that traditionally sap energy from cross-team initiatives.

Figure 4: The Data Catalyst3 Cycle

The same rotational model becomes indispensable during AI model development and lifecycle management. Governance ensures responsible use by defining criteria for data quality, model transparency, lineage, and risk thresholds. As covered in the AI governance considerations, this clarity is essential for ethical and auditable model use. Change management supports adoption by preparing business users, addressing fear, and countering AI-related myths with real stories and soundbites. And fluency ensures people understand how to interpret model outputs, recognize when the model is wrong, and make decisions that integrate human judgment with technical insight. Without this three-way rotation, AI models become compliance artifacts or technical curiosities rather than value-generating assets.

Even quarterly business routines benefit from this coordinated discipline rotation. Governance contributes monitored metrics, recurring decisions, and trust scores. Change management provides visibility into organizational sentiment and identifies early warning signs of adoption decline. Fluency adds analytical competence and ensures leaders interpret the data with the right context. The rotation creates a rhythm that prevents the organization from slipping back into old habits. Over time, these recurring loops reinforce the Momentum Flywheel outlined earlier in this section, where clarity drives adoption, adoption strengthens fluency, and fluency deepens trust. When the disciplines move independently, the flywheel slows. When they move together, the flywheel spins on its own.

The goal of integrating the disciplines is not to create more processes. The goal is to create more certainty, more alignment, and more trust—before work begins, while change is occurring, and after outcomes are delivered. The rotation of governance, change, and fluency becomes the operating choreography that allows teams to move confidently instead of reactively. It helps people understand not only what they are doing and why, but also how it connects to the behaviors that make the organization faster, safer, and smarter. When the three disciplines are used together, acceleration stops being episodic. It becomes the organization's natural state.

Scaling the Catalyst

Scaling shouldn't dilute the spark; it should amplify it. By the time you reach this point in the book, you've seen how Data Governance (through the Non-Invasive Data Governance approach), Change Management, and Data Fluency form the three catalytic forces that allow data and AI initiatives to move faster with far fewer surprises. You've also learned how the Data Catalyst[3] Spark Alignment Checklist gives you a clean, structured way to start, and how the Momentum Flywheel turns clarity, adoption, fluency, and trust into a self-reinforcing loop. But scaling is the moment where everything you've built transitions from "the first win" to "the way we work." And if you've ever seen a governance program lose momentum after a promising start, you already know how fragile that transition can be.

Scaling the Catalyst³ is not about replicating deliverables, artifacts, or tools like a franchise starter kit. It's about replicating the **conditions** that created early success. Quick wins happen because people are engaged, roles are clear, literacy gaps are acknowledged, resistance is addressed, and trust improves visibly. Scaling means ensuring those same conditions of clarity, accountability, context, capability, and confidence exist beyond the first team, the first project, or the first domain. It is not more work. It is the multiplication of the work that already works.

The first step in scaling is identifying your catalysts, which are your early champions. These are the people who didn't just participate; they **felt the impact**. They saw what happened when governance stopped being a compliance hammer and started being an accelerant. They saw what happened when change management wasn't a communication blast but a behavioral support system. They saw what happened when literacy wasn't a training course but a confidence booster. These individuals become the carriers of belief. They embody the SPARK before it has even been formally tested with the SPARK Test. Scaling begins by formalizing their involvement—recruiting them as advocates, using them as storytellers, and empowering them to mentor the next cohort of teams.

The second step is decentralizing execution while preserving accountability. Governance is most powerful when it is closest to the business domain, which is a core principle of Non-Invasive Data Governance. Scaling the Catalyst³ means distributing stewardship responsibilities, decision clarity, and literacy reinforcement into the natural flow of work. But decentralization without structure becomes chaos. This is why the Accountability Alignment Matrix becomes foundational in scaling: it clarifies who decides what, where data truth lives, and how escalations work across expanding surfaces of work. As the Catalyst³ approach grows, the matrix becomes your stabilizer, keeping decentralized work aligned with centralized strategy.

Stories are the third driver of scale. Data governance has historically suffered from a narrative problem: people only hear about governance when something goes wrong. The Catalyst³ approach fixes this by turning **value into visibility**. As described in the section about Changing the Narrative, stories become accelerants when they are packaged, repeated, and shared at the right cadence. To scale, you must replicate the storytelling routines that made your early wins believable. That might include "Catalyst Minutes" at leadership meetings, quarterly publication of before-and-after transformations, or internal interviews with practitioners describing what changed for them. These stories don't just share success; they normalize it.

Scaling also requires embedding Catalyst³ principles into the organizational "front door." That means modifying project intake forms so they automatically ask for data domains, accountability roles, expected behavior changes, and literacy requirements. It means adding Catalyst³ checkpoints to onboarding so new employees learn the glossary, the triad structure (governance–change–fluency), and the accountability pathways before they ever join a project team. It means ensuring performance expectations include data fluency competencies and reinforced governance behaviors. Scaling is successful when Catalyst principles show up before you remind people they exist.

Hazards of the Catalyst

Of course, scaling introduces hazards—five in particular. The first is **bureaucratic drift**, when well-intended teams add steps, checkpoints, and committees that slow everything down. The antidote is returning to the Non-Invasive principles: governance must be embedded, not bolted on; change must be supportive, not prescribed. The second hazard is **inconsistent adoption**, where teams apply pieces of the Catalyst³ approach out of order or skip foundational steps. The Integration Blueprint solves this by providing a predictable rotation: Align → Activate → Accelerate.

The third hazard is **role confusion**, when responsibilities become blurred as the approach spreads. Maintaining a clear Decision Rights Matrix prevents this. The fourth hazard is **tool fixation**, where organizations declare victory because they installed a platform, glossary, or dashboard. Tools support acceleration; they are not the acceleration. And the fifth hazard is **literacy decay**, when fluency training is treated as a one-time event rather than a continuous competency. You counter this by embedding fluency refreshers into ongoing routines rather than standalone courses.

Scaling becomes far less intimidating when it becomes intentional. The Catalyst³ approach gives you structure for that intention. You already have the spark—the quick wins, the clarity, the trust signals, the stories. Now you are extending that spark across teams and time without losing the energy that produced it. The role you play shifts from being the "initiator" of change to being the "amplifier" of change.

Scaling is the point at which Catalyst³ stops being something you do and becomes something **the organization** does. It's the moment when the practices, beliefs, and rhythms described throughout this book begin to stand on their own. And once they do, the spark no longer needs to be relit. It simply keeps spreading.

Steps to Sustain Acceleration

Acceleration becomes culture only when it becomes memory. Up to this point in the book, we've walked through the spark, the disciplines, the narrative shift, and the mechanics that turn intention into motion. But acceleration is fragile. Left unattended, it fades. Left undocumented, it gets rewritten. Left unreinforced, it slowly slides back toward the very inertia the Catalyst³ approach was designed to overcome. Sustaining acceleration is the work of turning the Catalyst from something you *do* into something your organization *is*.

The first step in sustaining acceleration is integrating Catalyst routines into the earliest moments of the employee experience. Onboarding is not merely administrative; it is identity-forming. Too many organizations wait months before introducing new team members to governance expectations, decision rights, or the glossary. By then, habits have already hardened, and ungoverned shortcuts have settled in. Sustaining acceleration means placing the triad of governance, change, and fluency directly into orientation. New employees should learn how data moves through the organization and what accountable behavior looks like before they ever touch a system or join a project. When Catalyst principles appear on Day One, people assume they were always there.

Sustaining the triad itself requires deliberate maintenance. A triad that launches well can just as easily drift apart if rhythms loosen or communication slows. The monthly reviews described in the Integration Blueprint must continue, and not as meetings to "check the box," but as checkpoints to ensure alignment, momentum, and balance across the three disciplines. Governance teams must continue to ask, "What decisions were hard last month?" Change practitioners must ask, "Where did resistance show up?" Fluency teams must ask, "Where was confidence lacking?" The triad is the organization's early-warning system, and sustaining acceleration means continuing to use it even when things are going well.

Refreshing literacy without overtraining is another essential discipline. Literacy is not a one-time certification; it's a living capability. But nothing kills enthusiasm faster than saturation. Sustaining acceleration means designing literacy refreshers that are lightweight, situation-specific, and embedded in the work itself. Short micro-stories tied to real data moments, quick "fluency checkpoints" before new AI features launch, or targeted refreshers scheduled around quarterly business cycles can maintain capability without overwhelming teams. The goal is progress, not proficiency badges.

Governance, too, must be protected from "enforcement creep." As the Catalyst[3] concept scales, governance can unintentionally become heavier, with more forms, reviews, and approvals. Sustaining acceleration means defending the Non-Invasive principles outlined in my other books. If governance begins to feel like a barrier rather than an accelerant, the organization will quietly route around it. The antidote is simple but powerful: keep governance embedded, contextual, and tied to outcomes. A quarterly "governance calibration," where leaders revisit decisions, friction points, and simplification opportunities, prevents drift and keeps governance aligned to the Catalyst's intent.

At the heart of sustaining acceleration is what I call **the Catalyst Memory**, which is the organizational memory of wins that reinforces belief. Organizations often forget their victories faster than their failures, especially when leadership changes or priorities shift. Sustaining acceleration means preserving and curating these wins with intention. This includes publishing value stories, tracking trust signals from the Momentum Flywheel, updating a running ledger of business impacts, and creating rituals that celebrate governed decisions, successful model launches, and literacy breakthroughs.

These rituals matter more than most organizations realize. A five-minute "Catalyst Story" at a department meeting, a quarterly "Acceleration Day" spotlighting improvements, or a simple showcase of data-supported decisions keeps the spark visible. When leaders repeatedly reinforce these stories publicly, the organization internalizes that acceleration is a feature of its identity, not a phase of its program.

As teams grow, roles shift, and new technologies introduce fresh challenges, the Catalyst Memory becomes the anchor keeping the organization grounded in what works. It provides historical continuity, especially when executives rotate or reorganizations take place. It ensures that progress does not depend on any single leader, but on a shared belief system shaped by evidence.

This Activation and Acceleration Guide is not about new frameworks or additional tools. Instead, it is about ensuring that what you learned in Sections One through Seven not only survives but also strengthens over time. If those earlier sections helped you reimagine data governance, change management, and data fluency for the age of AI, then this section ensures the narrative and the momentum endure.

The Executive Briefing Guide

Five-minute read.
Share with your leadership.

Light the fuse with
your leadership!

Executive Summary

We live in an era where speed, trust, and adaptability are no longer luxuries—they are requirements for survival. Executives face a world defined by disruption, where artificial intelligence (AI) promises transformation but also introduces new risks. Customer expectations rise faster than organizations can pivot, and regulators, investors, and boards demand greater accountability for how data is managed. In this climate, data governance is not optional. It is essential. But the way governance is introduced, sustained, and adopted makes the difference between success and failure.

The premise of *Data Catalyst³ (Cubed)* is simple yet powerful: data governance alone is not enough. Traditional approaches have struggled to gain traction because they have been delivered as mandates, imposed roles, and compliance projects that spark resistance rather than engagement. What organizations truly need is a catalyst—a spark that accelerates change rather than hindering it. That catalyst comes not from governance in isolation, but from the deliberate combination of three disciplines: Non-Invasive Data Governance (NIDG), Change Management, and Data Fluency (commonly referred to as Literacy). Together, these disciplines not only add value, but also multiply it.

For executives, the message is urgent: AI won't wait. Competitors won't wait. Culture won't wait. If governance is delayed, you risk building AI on untrustworthy data, losing market share to faster rivals, and cementing governance as a compliance function rather than a business accelerator. Acting now, with the Catalyst³ attitude, ensures that data becomes a competitive asset, that change is adopted with less resistance, and that literacy and fluency empowers people across the organization to use data confidently and responsibly.

This briefing distills the key lessons of *Data Catalyst³* for senior leaders. It explains why the spark is needed now, how the cubed effect works, what practical benefits it delivers, and, most importantly, what role executives must play in making it a reality. The goal is to provide you not only with an understanding of the framework but also with the conviction and urgency to act.

The Case for The Data Catalyst[3]: Why a Spark Is Needed

Business conditions are more volatile than ever. Supply chain disruptions, market instability, regulatory shifts, and rapid technology advances mean organizations cannot rely on predictability. Traditional governance approaches built around rigid control and top-down enforcement falter in this climate. What is required is agility—the ability to pivot quickly without sacrificing trust. The "spark" of Data Catalyst[3] provides exactly that—governance, change, and fluency working together as a stabilizing force in chaotic times.

Artificial intelligence has amplified the urgency. Many organizations are racing to deploy models trained on ungoverned, unvalidated data. This is a recipe for bias, failure, and reputational damage. The truth is simple: AI without governed data is a risk multiplier. Executives must recognize that governance is not an obstacle to AI, but the very foundation of trustworthy AI adoption. The spark of Catalyst[3] ensures AI is sustainable, auditable, and aligned with business value.

Trust in data is fragile. Executives hesitate to act when dashboards conflict. Managers lose faith when reports don't align. Practitioners create workarounds when systems don't match reality. Every governance failure erodes credibility, and rebuilding trust is a slow and costly process. Catalyst[3] reframes governance as the path back to trust—not through top-down enforcement, but through embedded accountability and shared fluency. Without the spark, skepticism persists and adoption stalls.

The speed of decisions is accelerating, but governance has often lagged behind. Executives are pressured to make real-time decisions, while governance processes built for quarterly reviews or committee approvals struggle to keep up. Catalyst[3] aligns governance practices with modern decision-making velocity. Definitions, stewardship, and literacy are woven into workflows so governance is in the flow of business rather than standing apart from it.

Finally, resistance fatigue is real. Organizations are tired of initiatives that over-promise and under-deliver. Data Catalyst³ combats this fatigue by reframing governance not as one more burden, but as an accelerator of existing priorities. By demonstrating quick wins and measurable improvements, Catalyst³ rebuilds energy and engagement where fatigue once reigned.

The Executive Power of the Catalyst

The power of Data Catalyst³ lies in multiplication. Governance, change management, and fluency each provide value on their own—accountability, adoption, and confidence. But when combined, their value multiplies. Governance provides structure, change management provides adoption, and fluency and literacy provides empowerment. Together, they accelerate trust, decision-making, and cultural transformation.

Executives must recognize this multiplier effect. Investing in one discipline alone is insufficient. Governance without change management is ignored. Change management without governance is empty theater. Fluency without governance is chaos. But cubed together, they create acceleration that no single discipline can achieve. This is why the framework is Catalyst³, not Catalyst².

The Data Catalyst³ in Practice

In practice, The Data Catalyst³ technique works by activating three disciplines—governance, change, and fluency—in a coordinated sequence that accelerates decision-making, reduces friction, and builds trust across the organization. The following narratives show how each discipline becomes a catalyst on its own, and how together they create the conditions for responsible, confident, and AI-ready execution.

Data Governance as a Catalyst

Governance is often misunderstood as control, compliance, and restriction. The Non-Invasive Data Governance approach reframes it as accountability without shackles. Instead of assigning new roles, NIDG recognizes existing accountabilities and formalizes them. Instead of imposing disruptive processes, it embeds governance into the work people already do. Instead of being perceived as "extra," it becomes the way business is done.

Executives benefit from alignment: decisions flow faster because accountability is clear. Managers benefit from efficiency: duplication and rework are reduced. Practitioners benefit from clarity: ownership and stewardship are known, definitions are consistent, and trust is built. Trust, in turn, unlocks adoption. No executive invests in data they don't trust. No manager relies on reports they doubt. No practitioner uses tools they don't believe in. Trust is the acceleration that governance provides.

Metrics seal the case. Executives fund what they can measure. Catalyst[3] governance demonstrates its value through metrics that resonate—fewer errors, faster projects, smoother audits, and more reliable AI. Metrics shift governance from theory to evidence, ensuring sustainable support at every level.

Change Management as a Catalyst

Governance fails when change is ignored. Resistance is inevitable, but it is not a sign of failure—it is a sign of energy. Catalyst[3] treats resistance as fuel, guiding adoption instead of fighting it. Executives must learn to respect resistance, managers must channel it into improvement, and practitioners must see it as their chance to contribute.

Adoption requires psychology. People don't change because they are told to. They change when they feel ownership, fairness, and competence. Catalyst[3] addresses these psychological drivers by distributing accountability, clarifying roles, and building confidence through literacy. Executives can model adoption by using governed data in their own decisions. Managers can reinforce it by embedding governance into team practices. Practitioners can live it daily by sharing wins and flagging issues.

Momentum is built through small wins, not big-bang rollouts. Micro-changes reassure people that governance works. Stories amplify those wins, spreading belief more effectively than policies. Distributed leadership multiplies impact, ensuring governance is carried by champions throughout the business, not just by one sponsor at the top.

Data Fluency as a Catalyst

Fluency is the multiplier that makes governance and change management stick. Without fluency, governance remains abstract and adoption collapses. Fluency ensures that executives can question data with confidence, managers can collaborate without bottlenecks, and practitioners can apply data responsibly in their daily work.

Fluency matters more than expertise. Not everyone needs to be a data scientist, but everyone needs to be fluent enough to participate. Raising the baseline across the organization ensures inclusion and scalability. Shared language breaks barriers, enabling cross-functional collaboration. Confidence drives participation, reducing the fear that keeps people silent in data discussions.

Fluency and literacy must be practical. One-off training doesn't stick. Programs tied to real work and real data create fluency that endures. When governance and literacy are integrated, fluency accelerates adoption naturally. The result is an organization where data is no longer intimidating, but empowering.

The Leadership Imperative

Executives cannot delegate Data Catalyst³. Sponsorship is not enough; leadership must actively champion, model, and demand it. The role of leadership is to set tone, align priorities, and tell stories that position governance as an accelerator rather than a cost.

Role-Based Actions

- **CEOs** must integrate governance into strategy, making it inseparable from growth, innovation, and AI adoption. Their words and actions signal to the enterprise whether governance is a side project or a core enabler.

- **CIOs** must partner with governance to ensure technology investments deliver ROI. IT has historically consumed the bulk of data-related budgets, but without governance, those investments underperform. CIOs must embrace governance as the missing multiplier.

- **CFOs and CROs** must see governance as risk management. Financial controls, compliance, and regulatory obligations cannot be trusted without governed data. Governance reduces financial and reputational exposure.

- **CDOs, CDAOs, and CDAIOs** must operationalize Data Catalyst[3]. As stewards of data and AI, they must ensure governance is embedded, change is managed, and fluency is grown. Their leadership ensures governance scales beyond IT and into the business.

Managers must operationalize executive vision, embedding governance into daily workflows. Practitioners must live the change, formalizing the accountability they already hold. Everyone must be data-woke, recognizing that their daily interactions with data contribute to trust. Distributed ownership sustains governance, ensuring no one role carries it alone.

Shifting the Narrative

Executives must also recognize their role in changing the narrative. Words matter. Selling governance as compliance sells pain. Selling governance as a catalyst sells value. Executives buy speed, managers buy efficiency, practitioners buy clarity. Governance framed as an accelerator resonates with each audience.

The AI era raises the stakes. If governance is framed as optional, AI risks multiply. If it is framed as essential, AI becomes trusted and scalable. Stories spread faster than policies. Executives must become storytellers, sharing wins and reinforcing governance as a catalyst in every strategic conversation.

Executive Call to Action and Conclusion

The case is clear: Action cannot wait. AI is scaling faster than governance. Trust is fragile and erodes with every failure. Competitors are already gaining an advantage with governed data. Culture, once set, is difficult to reset. Momentum multiplies only when it is built, not when it is delayed.

Catalyst³ provides the roadmap: governance for accountability, change management for adoption, fluency for empowerment. Together, they create acceleration that no single discipline can achieve. Executives must seize this moment to position governance not as an afterthought, but as a catalyst for everything that matters—AI, transformation, compliance, growth, and trust.

The challenge is direct: Share this message with your leadership team. Embed governance into your strategy. Demand metrics that prove acceleration. Celebrate wins that build trust. And most importantly, act now.

AI won't wait. Neither should you.

The
Data Catalyst^3
Field Guide

Tools to accelerate a reaction!

Canvases to light the spark!

Lighting the Spark: Matchbook and Ignition

The Matchbooks to Spark the Catalyst

One of the consistent challenges organizations face when it comes to governance, change, and fluency is the jump from *concept* to *action*. You can read about frameworks, hear stories of success, or nod in agreement at the logic, but unless there's a way to put these ideas into play on the ground, the spark never catches. That is why this section exists. It is designed to give you something tangible, usable, and ready to deploy tomorrow morning.

These five Canvases, drawn from the core sections of this book, are not theory. They are practical canvases you can carry into a meeting, hang on a whiteboard, or fill out in a workshop with your team. Each one addresses a critical piece of awakening Data Catalyst³: igniting momentum, clarifying accountability, sequencing wins, building fluency, and reframing the story. Each one is simple enough to be non-invasive yet structured enough to produce value that you can show to your executives.

To make them truly useful, I've included:

- A description of what the Canvas captures and why it matters.

- Guidance on how to gather the inputs.

- A Field Guide for recording the inputs.

- Examples, only the fields that most often confuse, to help you avoid the traps that stall adoption.

Think of these as matchbooks. Each Canvas is a way to strike a flame. Used together, they will help you light the fire of governance, change, and literacy in your organization.

Why I Use the Expression Canvas

The reason I use the term "Canvas" rather than "Tool" or "Template" is very intentional. In academic and design-thinking circles, a canvas has come to represent a structured, visual framework that helps people think strategically, align ideas, and capture inputs in a way that feels more collaborative than prescriptive. Think of the popular Business Model Canvas—it doesn't dictate answers, it invites exploration. By framing the artifacts in this book as canvases, the emphasis shifts away from filling in forms or checking boxes and toward guiding meaningful conversations that lead to action. A tool suggests something rigid or mechanical, and a template suggests something to be completed once and filed away. A canvas, on the other hand, is about ongoing creativity, clarity, and adaptability.

The metaphor of a canvas also perfectly reflects the act of starting with a clean slate while still being provided with structure. Just like an artist approaches a blank canvas with both freedom and boundaries, organizations can use these canvases to bring order to complex, messy topics without stifling the unique context of their situation. The structure is there—fields, categories, and prompts—but what gets written, drawn, or mapped into that structure is always organization-specific. This makes canvases far more flexible than templates, because they encourage iteration. Teams can return to the canvas again and again, adding new layers as strategies evolve, as if layering paint to create depth.

Finally, the word "canvas" conveys a sense of shared ownership. Tools are often handed down from above, and templates are often pushed out as compliance artifacts, but canvases invite people from all levels of the organization to participate in shaping the picture. The process of filling in a canvas naturally sparks collaboration and discussion, which is exactly the spirit of Non-Invasive Governance. A canvas is not about control—it's about framing a dialogue, surfacing insights, and helping people see how their contributions fit into the bigger picture. For that reason, the word *canvas* doesn't just describe what these artifacts are, it describes how they work: structured spaces where governance, change, and literacy come together to create clarity and momentum.

Igniting the Catalyst –The Spark Alignment Checklist (Canvas for Section 2)

When organizations consider igniting momentum for governance, change management, and fluency, the conversation often shifts toward technology, tools, or large-scale initiatives. But the real spark begins not with budgets or platforms, but with alignment. Without clarity about what matters, energy disperses like smoke rather than fueling the kind of fire that drives transformation. That is why a Spark Alignment Checklist becomes such a powerful artifact. It is not flashy or complicated. It is practical, tangible, and, when used consistently, capable of turning scattered good intentions into a focused blaze of results.

The Spark Alignment Checklist is about validation. It ensures that every initiative connected to data, AI, and governance begins by asking the right questions. Are accountabilities clarified? Are resistance points surfaced and acknowledged? Are literacy and fluency needs identified for every role that matters? Are executives aware of how this initiative ties directly to organizational strategy? When these questions are answered with confidence, the chances of success increase dramatically. When they are left vague or ignored, projects stumble, fatigue spreads, and the culture becomes skeptical that governance ever delivers value.

Think of the checklist as striking a match. A match on its own will flare briefly and then fizzle out. But when struck against the right surface, with dry tinder waiting to catch fire, it creates a flame that warms and endures. In the same way, the checklist forces practitioners to strike against reality. It is not enough to say that people will "probably" know their roles or "should" trust the data. The checklist requires confirmation. Without this discipline, efforts may appear impressive on paper but ultimately fail to deliver in practice.

For executives, the Spark Alignment Checklist becomes a confidence-building tool. They often worry that governance programs are disconnected from strategy or weighed down with bureaucracy. Showing them that each initiative is tested against strategic alignment, resistance readiness, and literacy integration reframes governance as disciplined and agile. It reassures them that resources will not be wasted chasing after another project that burns out quickly. For managers, the checklist reduces duplication and frustration. They no longer need to chase down definitions or second-guess roles because accountability was tested at the start. For practitioners, it builds trust. They can see that governance is not "one more thing" but a way to reduce the time they spend reconciling reports, chasing definitions, and fighting system mismatches.

The Spark Alignment Checklist also scales across projects. It can be applied to a massive AI rollout, where executives must know the data is trustworthy and explainable, or to a departmental dashboard refresh, where managers want to ensure reports reconcile without endless firefighting. The point is not the size of the project. The point is the consistency of the spark. Each use of the checklist sets fire to fatigue and replaces it with energy and alignment.

Skeptics may dismiss a checklist as too simple. But simplicity is the point. In an environment of constant disruption, people do not need another heavy methodology. They need clarity in the moment. They need to know the basics are covered so they can move with speed. A Spark Alignment Checklist is not about bureaucracy; it is about acceleration. And when used with discipline, it becomes a cultural artifact. Teams expect it. Leaders ask for it. Over time, it shapes behavior so thoroughly that alignment becomes muscle memory.

In practice, the Spark Alignment Checklist is a living artifact, not a static document. It evolves as the organization matures. Early versions may be short and basic: Are roles identified? Is leadership aware? Are definitions documented? Later versions may become more nuanced, asking about data lineage, AI model validation, or literacy baselines. The growth of the checklist reflects the growth of the culture. The important part is that it always focuses on alignment, clarity, and ignition.

By incorporating this checklist into their governance practices, organizations demonstrate that they are serious about minimizing energy waste. They demonstrate that governance is not about compliance or bureaucracy but about achieving meaningful results. For practitioners, it serves as a guardrail that keeps them from straying off course. For managers, it is the assurance that efforts will not collapse under confusion. For executives, it is the reassurance that governance delivers acceleration, not delay.

The Spark Alignment Checklist is the first artifact because it is the first act of discipline. Without it, organizations chase sparks that never catch. With it, they light fires that transform data, AI, and culture. And once the fire begins, the warmth of trust and the light of alignment spread through the organization in ways that cannot be ignored.

Canvas Development and Use

Every organization says they want to move faster with data and AI, but speed without control quickly becomes chaos. The Spark Alignment Checklist is designed to be the ignition point that ensures governance, change management, and fluency aren't bolted on after the fact, but instead are baked into the DNA of every initiative. It's not about slowing projects down. It's about creating the conditions for sustainable acceleration—the kind that scales, survives leadership changes, and earns trust rather than burning it.

By using this readiness canvas at the start of a project, you can align effort with the enterprise strategy, assign accountability upfront, identify adoption risks before they derail momentum, and define quick-win proof that executives can rally behind. It's simple, visible, and non-invasive—but it has the power to shift a project from "just another initiative" into a catalyst for broader organizational change.

How to Gather the Inputs

1. **Interview the executive sponsor for the business outcome, hard success metrics, and decision deadlines.** This is where you get beyond vague goals like "improve efficiency" and instead pin down measurable outcomes, such as reducing a cycle time by 20% or increasing forecast accuracy by five

percentage points. Having an executive voice, these metrics anchor the initiative in accountability and urgency.

2. **Facilitate a short workshop with managers and practitioners to identify impacted data domains, named owners, and trust issues.** These are the people closest to the work, and they'll quickly tell you where data is unreliable, where definitions clash, and where ownership is murky. Surfacing these insights early makes governance less about rules and more about solving real frustrations.

3. **Review systems and dashboards to confirm data lineage and baseline figures.** Don't rely solely on what people say— validate where data is coming from, how it flows, and what today's numbers look like. This establishes a baseline that can later prove whether your governance actions made a measurable difference.

4. **Run a light adoption scan (who must change what, by when) and a literacy check (role-based fluency needs).** Even the cleanest data and most brilliant AI won't stick if people don't adjust their behaviors. Identify early where training is needed, who will feel the changes most directly, and what kind of support will help them succeed.

5. **Agree on one quick win in less than 60 days and the evidence you will publish to prove value.** Projects live or die on momentum. By delivering a small but visible success quickly, you buy credibility with leadership and reduce skepticism among practitioners. Equally important: decide how and where you'll communicate that win, so it spreads beyond the immediate project team.

Canvas Field Guide

- **Initiative**: The project or AI use case that needs acceleration. It should be described clearly enough that anyone in the organization can understand the purpose and intended outcome. The goal here is to avoid the common pitfall of "fuzzy initiatives" that sound strategic but lack a clear definition.

- **Outcome and Metric**: The concrete result and measurement you are pursuing, from baseline to target. This forces a move from aspiration to accountability. Without a clear metric, governance efforts risk being perceived as abstract rather than value-generating.

- **Strategic Link**: The enterprise priority or OKR (Objectives and Key Results) that the initiative supports. By anchoring governance actions to existing strategic goals, you reduce resistance and increase executive visibility. If an initiative cannot be linked to strategy, it's worth asking whether it deserves governance attention at all.

- **Data Domains**: The subject areas most impacted by the initiative. Being explicit about domains prevents surprises later when teams discover that critical data sets were overlooked. Identifying these early also helps you engage the right stewards.

- **Governance Accountability**: The named roles who own definitions and quality for the data. This is not about assigning new work but recognizing where accountability already exists. It formalizes relationships that are often assumed but rarely documented.

- **Change Risks**: The risks to adoption, such as identity, fairness, or workload issues. Many governance initiatives fail not because the data is wrong but because people feel threatened or overloaded. Capturing risks here makes it easier to build mitigation strategies before they become roadblocks.

- **Literacy Gaps**: The role-based fluency needs that must be addressed for the initiative to succeed. This ensures governance doesn't just fix the data but equips people to use it with confidence. It highlights the training or support that will be required.

- **Trust Score (0–5)**: A subjective but powerful rating of how much people currently trust the data. Tracking this score over time provides a quick health check of cultural progress, and it reinforces that trust is as important a metric as technical quality.

- **Quick Win**: A deliverable that can be achieved in sixty days or less to prove acceleration. This field forces prioritization and keeps the team focused on results that generate belief. It's better to deliver a small but visible success than to aim for perfection that never arrives.

- **Evidence and Comms**: The plan for how success will be published and communicated. This ensures wins are not hidden in a corner but shared in ways that inspire replication across the organization. Governance gains credibility when it is seen, not just done.

Canvas Ignitor

The Spark Alignment Checklist is your ignition point. It ensures that governance, change management, and fluency are not afterthoughts but designed into the very start of an initiative.

Sample Canvas Layout

- **Columns**: Initiative, Outcome and Metric, Strategic Link, Governance Accountability, Change Risks, Literacy Gaps, Trust Score, Quick Win, Evidence and Comms.

- **Rows**: Each initiative being evaluated.

Example (highlighting fields that confuse most):

Initiative	Outcome and Metric	Governance Accountability	Change Risks	Trust Score (0–5)	Quick Win
AI Next-Best-Offer	+3% conversion in 90 days	Marketing steward, Product steward	Sales pushback (Medium)	2	Single-offer pilot segment
Customer 360 Cleanup	Reduce duplicate IDs by 40%	CRM Admin, Data Quality Steward	Ops workload concerns (L)	3	Dedup rule on top sources
ESG Data Automation	Cut reporting cycle by 30%	Risk steward, Finance steward	Fear of scrutiny (Medium)	2	Automate two ESG metrics
Forecast Accuracy	Improve MAPE 24% → 18%	Ops and Inventory Stewards	Skepticism (High)	1	Clean promo calendar feed
Expense Analytics	Shorten variance analysis cycle by 25%	Finance and Procurement Stewards	Shadow spreadsheets (High)	2	Standardize definitions

Data Governance as a Catalyst –The Accountability Alignment Matrix (Canvas for Section 3)

One of the greatest misconceptions about governance is that it requires authority. Leaders imagine new roles, titles, or committees created to enforce compliance. Practitioners often dread the bureaucracy that is layered on top of their work. Managers fear duplication and confusion. But the truth is that accountability already exists. People are already defining, producing, and using data. They are already accountable for the quality of their outputs and the decisions made from their inputs. The problem is that accountability is hidden, inconsistent, or misunderstood. That is why the Accountability Alignment Matrix is such a critical artifact. It does not invent accountability. It reveals it.

The Accountability Alignment Matrix is a simple yet transformative tool that maps critical data domains and processes against existing roles. It makes explicit what has long been implicit. Who is accountable for the customer master? Who decides when a definition of revenue changes? Who ensures that product data remains consistent across the supply chain and sales systems? These questions are often answered informally, creating confusion when problems arise. The matrix removes ambiguity by laying out accountability clearly and visibly.

For executives, this artifact brings alignment. They no longer need to suffer through meetings where different leaders present conflicting metrics and no one knows who is responsible. The matrix shows exactly where accountability sits, who owns definitions, and who is responsible for ensuring quality. This alignment accelerates decision-making because it removes the friction of confusion. For managers, the matrix reduces duplication. It prevents multiple teams from working on the same problem without realizing it. For practitioners, it provides clarity. They know who to go to when questions arise and who will back them up when data is challenged.

The power of the Accountability Alignment Matrix lies in its non-invasive nature. It does not assign new titles or create artificial roles.

Instead, it recognizes the accountability people already have through their relationship to data. A CRM administrator already has influence over customer data. A supply chain analyst already ensures product data is accurate. A marketing analyst already reconciles campaign data. The matrix formalizes this reality, making it visible and consistent. By doing so, it builds trust without disruption.

Critics may say that mapping accountability is too basic, but they overlook the cost of not doing so. When accountability is unclear, executives lose confidence in data, projects stall, and frustration builds. Every hour wasted reconciling reports or debating definitions is an hour lost to decision-making. The matrix prevents this waste. It transforms governance from being seen as a burden into being recognized as a time-saver.

Over time, the Accountability Alignment Matrix becomes a cultural anchor. It shapes behavior because people know their responsibilities are visible and consistent. It becomes a reference point for onboarding, audits, and AI projects alike. New employees quickly learn where accountability sits. Regulators see clarity rather than chaos. AI models are trained on governed data because accountability for definitions and quality was clarified before deployment.

The matrix also scales with organizational maturity. In early stages, it may only map a handful of critical domains: customer, product, revenue. Later, it can expand to include dozens of processes and subdomains. The point is not the size of the matrix. The point is the clarity it creates. By making accountability visible, the matrix accelerates decision-making, reduces duplication, and builds trust.

Executives care about results, not theory. When they see that a simple matrix prevents the embarrassment of conflicting reports or the delay of stalled projects, they understand the value. Managers appreciate the efficiency gained from eliminating confusion. Practitioners appreciate the clarity that helps them focus on delivering value rather than chasing down answers. In every case, the Accountability Alignment Matrix demonstrates that governance is not about control. It is about acceleration.

Canvas Development and Use

In most organizations, accountability for data is assumed but never made explicit. People work around one another, decisions get delayed, and executives are left wondering why the same arguments resurface in every meeting. The Accountability and Decision Rights Matrix exists to cut through this ambiguity. It reveals where accountability already sits, rather than creating new roles, and it clarifies how decisions actually get made.

The point is not bureaucracy; it is alignment. By making the RACI (Responsible, Accountable, Consulted, Informed) roles visible, and by adding Decision Authority (DAI), the matrix becomes a practical tool for ensuring that governance accelerates rather than obstructs. With it, projects can move faster, people know where to go for answers, and leadership has confidence that escalations will be resolved consistently and fairly.

How to Gather the Inputs

1. **Extract data domains and processes from current projects and reports.** Look at the most active initiatives, recurring reporting packages, and systems of record to build a list of domains and processes. This ensures the matrix covers what is relevant today rather than creating an abstract catalog.

2. **Identify critical decisions from escalation history and audit items.** Review where disagreements, delays, or audit findings have occurred in the past. These are the moments where accountability was unclear and documenting them ensures the matrix solves real pain points.

3. **Interview domain owners to map R/A/C/I and Decision Authority.** Engage the people who already manage or steward

the data. Walk through each critical decision and record who takes action, who is ultimately accountable, who must be consulted, and who needs to be informed. Then capture who actually holds the final say.

4. **Validate systems of record and controls with IT and risk functions.** Data accountability is not just about people; it's also about systems. Confirm which platforms are considered authoritative for each domain and document the policies, quality rules, and lineage that support them. This creates evidence that stands up in audits.

5. **Finalize escalation paths with the governance council.** Once the draft roles and decisions are captured, review them with your governance council or equivalent body. They can confirm how unresolved issues will escalate and the service-level expectations for turnaround. This closes the loop and makes the matrix operational.

Canvas Field Guide

- **Domain/Process**: The subject area being governed (e.g., Customer Master, Product Hierarchy). Naming the domain keeps the scope clear and prevents disputes over "who owns what."

- **Critical Decision**: The decision point that frequently causes conflict or delay (e.g., how duplicate records are handled). Capturing these prevents endless re-litigation of the same issues.

- **R / A / C / I**: The roles responsible, accountable, consulted, and informed for each decision. Making these visible prevents duplication of work and ensures clarity about who needs to be involved.

- **Decision Authority (D)**: The individual or role with the final say. Documenting this avoids paralysis and helps the organization move forward even in the face of disagreement.

- **Systems of Record**: The authoritative system where the truth is mastered. This prevents multiple versions of the truth from undermining trust and accelerates data reconciliation.

- **Controls/Evidence**: The policies, lineage, or quality rules tied to the domain. This ensures that decisions are backed by more than opinion and can stand up to external review.

- **KQIs/KPIs Owned**: The key metrics governed by this domain. Documenting them makes accountability measurable and ensures alignment between data and business outcomes.

- **Escalation Path**: The route unresolved issues take. Defining this means problems don't linger or get lost in organizational limbo.

- **SLA**: The turnaround expectation for decisions or escalations. By setting and honoring SLAs, governance gains credibility as a business enabler rather than a bottleneck.

Canvas Ignitor

Accountability without clarity is chaos. This matrix makes visible the people who already hold responsibility for data decisions and formalizes how those decisions get made.

Sample Canvas Layout

- **Columns**: Domain/Process, Critical Decision, Accountable Role, Decision Authority, Escalation Path, SLA.

- **Rows**: Each data domain or process.

Examples (fields that confuse most):

Domain/ Process	Critical Decision	Accountable Role	Decision Authority	Escalation Path	SLA
Customer Master	Golden record survivorship rule	Marketing Dir	Marketing Dir	DG Council → CDO	5 biz days
Product Hierarchy	Category merge/split approval	COO	COO	Ops Board → COO	3 biz days
Revenue Definition	Net versus Gross reporting	CFO	CFO	Finance SteerCo → CFO	7 biz days
Access Rights	PII viewing permission	CRO	CRO	Risk Committee → CRO	2 biz days
Forecast Inputs	Promo calendar acceptance	VP Ops	VP Ops	Ops SteerCo → COO	4 biz days

Change Management as a Catalyst –
The Momentum Map (Canvas for Section 4)

Change is often misunderstood as a one-time event. Leaders announce a new program, managers roll out new processes, and practitioners are expected to adapt immediately. However, change does not work that way. It is not a switch flipped in a single moment. It is a journey of momentum, built one win at a time. That is why the Momentum Map is such a powerful artifact. It is a plan for building and sustaining energy through a series of deliberate, visible victories.

The Momentum Map is about sequencing. It recognizes that large transformations overwhelm people, while small wins reassure them. It charts a path from early, low-risk wins to larger, more complex changes. Each win builds confidence, reduces resistance, and proves that governance accelerates results. Without such a map, organizations lurch from initiative to initiative, exhausting people and eroding trust. With it, they create a rhythm of progress that becomes unstoppable.

For executives, the Momentum Map provides visibility. They can see how small wins connect to larger outcomes, making it easier to justify investment. For managers, it provides pacing. They can manage workload and resistance by focusing on achievable milestones. For practitioners, it provides reassurance. They no longer face overwhelming change but a sequence of improvements that demonstrate value quickly.

The Momentum Map is not theoretical. It is practical and tangible. Stage one might involve cleaning up duplicate customer records to speed up onboarding. Stage two might involve reconciling definitions of revenue across departments. Stage three might involve embedding governance into AI model training. Each stage builds on the last, proving value while preparing for bigger challenges. The map makes progress visible, which is essential for sustaining momentum.

Change fatigue is real. People grow tired of endless initiatives that promise transformation but deliver frustration. The Momentum Map combats fatigue by demonstrating that governance is not an additional burden, but rather a series of accelerators. Each win is celebrated, each improvement is communicated, and each step forward reinforces the belief that change is working. Over time, the map becomes a cultural artifact, shaping how change is approached across the organization.

Critics may dismiss momentum as soft or intangible, but they misunderstand its power. Momentum is what carries organizations through resistance and uncertainty. It is what convinces skeptics to become believers. It is what transforms governance from a compliance exercise into a cultural movement. The Momentum Map is the artifact that ensures momentum is not left to chance but built intentionally and sustained deliberately.

Canvas Development and Use

One of the biggest mistakes organizations make with data governance, change initiatives, and fluency programs is aiming for perfection from the outset. Grand, sweeping transformations sound good in theory but quickly collapse under the weight of competing priorities and human resistance. The Momentum Map flips that script by focusing on small wins that build credibility, one success at a time.

This artifact helps you design a sequenced path where each win compounds into the next. By documenting hypotheses, baselines, targets, champions, and communication plans, it transforms progress into proof. Each win becomes a story worth sharing, and those stories are what build belief across the organization. Over time, the accumulation of quick wins adds up to cultural momentum that no executive speech or policy document could ever generate.

How to Gather the Inputs

1. **Review backlog and pain logs to select low-risk, high-visibility wins.** Go back through project backlogs, audit findings, and "known pain points" that staff complain about. Choosing items that can be fixed quickly will be visible to

stakeholders and won't require heavy funding or approvals to get started.

2. **Define hypotheses, baseline, and targets for each win.** Don't just "fix something"; articulate why fixing it matters. Capture the current state (baseline), what you expect to improve (target), and the hypothesis that links the improvement to business value. This turns each win into a measurable experiment rather than a vague improvement.

3. **Assign a champion and comms plan.** Every win needs someone visibly accountable to make it happen, as well as a plan for how results will be communicated. By naming both up front, you reduce the risk of wins going unnoticed or momentum fizzling after delivery.

4. **Record dependencies and scale criteria to unlock the next.** Think of the Momentum Map as a staircase: each win should make the next step easier. Document what must be true before you move forward, as well as how the win will be scaled or adapted for broader use.

5. **Publish results and harvest short stories for proof.** Wins that stay locked inside a project team don't build momentum across the enterprise. Publish before/after metrics, document the story of what was fixed, and share it widely. Stories travel faster than data and inspire the next wave of adoption.

Canvas Field Guide

- **Stage and Win**: The sequence and description of the improvement. Sequence is important because it ensures progress feels intentional rather than random, and each step builds toward a larger outcome.

- **Hypothesis of Value**: A short statement of why this particular win matters. It forces teams to articulate the "so what?" and link technical fixes to business impact.

- **Baseline → Target**: The improvement goal expressed as a measurable shift from today's state to the desired state. This provides evidence that governance and change aren't abstract—they deliver quantifiable progress.

- **Value Type and Method**: The type of value being created (time saved, cost reduced, risk mitigated, revenue improved) and how it will be measured. This ensures stakeholders understand the tangible business case.

- **Dates**: The start and end of the improvement cycle. Keeping these short prevents "never-ending pilots" and reinforces the idea that quick wins are achievable in weeks, not years.

- **Dependencies**: The prerequisites that must be satisfied before a win can succeed. Making them explicit avoids wasted effort on improvements that will collapse without the right foundation.

- **Champion**: The leader or steward accountable for making the win happen. By naming a visible champion, you create ownership and increase the likelihood that the win will be delivered.

- **Comms Plan**: The channels and cadence through which progress and results will be shared. A strong comms plan ensures that the credibility earned doesn't vanish into silence.

- **Story?** A record of whether the win has been captured and published as a narrative. Stories amplify metrics by making them relatable and repeatable.

- **Next Win**: The improvement that this one unlocks. This field ensures that momentum compounds rather than stalling, making each step a launchpad rather than an endpoint.

Canvas Ignitor

Big bang rollouts fail. Momentum maps succeed by accumulating small wins, demonstrating value early, and transforming success into compelling stories.

Sample Canvas Layout

- **Columns**: Stage and Win, Hypothesis of Value, Baseline → Target, Champion, Comms Plan, Next Win.

- **Rows**: Each sequential win.

Examples (fields that confuse most):

Stage and Win	Hypothesis of Value	Baseline → Target	Champion	Comms Plan	Next Win
Stage 1: Active Customer Def.	Reduce meeting friction	5 defs → 1	VP Marketing	Town hall + intranet	Stage 2
Stage 2: Deduplicate IDs	Improve campaign reach and CX	7% → 4% dupes	CRM Lead	Weekly dashboard	Stage 3
Stage 3: Stewardship Pilot	Reduce escalations	10/mo → 4/mo	DG Lead	Ops review bi-weekly	Stage 4
Stage 4: Order Quality Rules	Cut error corrections	1.8% → 0.9%	Ops Manager	Exec dashboard tile	Stage 5
Stage 5: Exec KPI Dashboard	Shared view builds trust	Trust 2.6 → 3.6	CDAO	Board deck updates	Scale BU

Data Fluency as a Catalyst –The Shared Language Glossary Canvas (Canvas for Section 5)

One of the most common sources of friction in organizations is the use of language. Executives, managers, and practitioners often use the exact words but mean different things. "Customer," "revenue," "active user"— these terms may sound simple, but they can create endless confusion when their definitions differ across silos. That is why the Shared Language Glossary Canvas is such a valuable artifact. It provides a lightweight, practical way to align language and reduce friction.

The glossary is not meant to be a heavy, bureaucratic metadata repository. It is a business-friendly, evolving document that captures the most critical terms, their definitions, and their ownership. Each department contributes, conflicts are surfaced, and reconciliation happens transparently. The glossary becomes a living artifact that enables faster decisions, reduces wasted time, and builds confidence in data.

For executives, the glossary provides clarity. They can trust that when reports show revenue, everyone is talking about the same thing. For managers, it reduces conflict. They no longer waste time reconciling conflicting definitions. For practitioners, it provides confidence. They can use data without fear of embarrassment because definitions are clear and consistent.

The Shared Language Glossary Canvas also supports AI initiatives. Models trained on data with inconsistent definitions produce unreliable results. By clarifying definitions, the glossary ensures that AI models are built on trustworthy data. This reduces risk and increases confidence in the adoption of AI.

Over time, the glossary becomes part of the organizational culture. It is referenced in meetings, included in onboarding, and used as a source of truth across projects. It reduces friction, builds trust, and accelerates collaboration. Critics may argue that a glossary is too simple, but simplicity is the point. People need practical tools they can use daily, not theoretical frameworks that gather dust. The glossary provides that practicality.

Canvas Development and Use

When organizations discuss being "data-driven," the conversation often derails before it even begins. Why? Because people can't even agree on what the words mean. Simple phrases like "customer," "revenue," or "engagement" can carry wildly different definitions depending on who you ask. A lightweight, business-owned glossary is one of the most effective tools for eliminating confusion, reducing risk, and building confidence in data conversations.

This artifact is not about building an academic dictionary that sits on a shelf. Instead, it is about providing businesspeople with a simple, shared language they can use on a day-to-day basis. By capturing clear definitions, rules, and ownership, the glossary becomes a living reference point for AI, analytics, and governance efforts. With each new definition clarified, the organization removes friction and creates a foundation of trust—something essential for accelerating outcomes at scale.

How to Gather the Inputs

1. **Ask each business area for their top 10 confusing or critical terms.** Start small by collecting a short list from every domain—not every possible word. Focusing on the terms that cause the most conflict or confusion ensures the glossary addresses real problems rather than being overwhelmed by low-value entries.

2. **Reconcile conflicts with stewards and Finance/Legal.** Many terms carry financial or compliance implications, and misalignment here can be costly. Involve data stewards, Finance, and Legal early on to harmonize conflicts and ensure every definition can withstand audit scrutiny.

3. **Add formula, systems of record, thresholds, and security class.** A glossary isn't just words on a page; it should include formulas, the authoritative system where the data lives, any thresholds for data quality, and its sensitivity classification. This prevents ambiguity and provides clear operational guidance.

4. **Capture simple examples and tag related terms.** People learn more effectively when they see examples, rather than just abstract rules. Tagging synonyms or conflicts between terms ensures that the glossary helps users resolve confusion rather than stumble into it.

5. **Publish with a review cycle.** A glossary is only trusted if it stays fresh. Assign ownership, set review dates, and commit to publishing updates regularly so the glossary becomes a living tool rather than another forgotten artifact.

Canvas Field Guide

- **Term**: The word or phrase in everyday use. Keeping it business-oriented ensures the glossary is helpful in non-technical staff.

- **Plain Definition**: A simple, jargon-free description. This should be written in language a new employee could understand without prior context.

- **Formula/Rule**: The explicit calculation or criteria behind the definition. Including this removes the guesswork and prevents competing formulas from creeping in.

- **Owner/Steward**: The accountable role or person who ensures the definition stays correct. This makes accountability visible rather than implied.

- **Systems/Lineage**: Where the data originates and how it flows. By making lineage explicit, organizations improve trust and reduce disputes over data sources.

- **Quality Threshold**: The acceptable rule for data quality (e.g., 98% completeness). This sets expectations and prevents debates over whether the data is "good enough."

- **Security Class**: The sensitivity rating of the data (e.g., Public, Internal, Confidential). Capturing this alongside the definition avoids accidental misuse.

- **Usage Contexts**: The business processes or reports where the term is applied. This helps people understand not only what the word means but also where it matters most.

- **Related/Conflicts**: Synonyms, similar terms, or known conflicts. By documenting them, you help users quickly navigate and resolve overlap.

- **Last Review/Version**: The review date and version number for auditability. This ensures executives and regulators that the glossary is subject to formal governance.

- **Example**: A concrete instance or sample record. Examples reduce ambiguity and make abstract definitions tangible.

Canvas Ignitor

Words make or break trust. This glossary makes sure everyone means the same thing when they say "customer," "revenue," or "risk."

Sample Canvas Layout

- **Columns**: Term, Definition, Formula/Rule, Owner/Steward, Example.

- **Rows**: Each high-value or high-conflict term.

Examples (fields that confuse most):

Term	Plain Definition	Formula/Rule	Owner/Steward	Example
Customer	Entity with a purchase in 24 months	Order ≥1 in the last 24 months	Marketing	Acme Co., order 11/15/24
Active Product	SKU with sales in 90 days	Sales > 0 in 90 days	Supply	SKU-4412
Net Revenue	Revenue after discounts/returns	Gross—Discounts—Returns	Finance	$12.4M May net
Active User	User session in the last 30 days	Session ≥1 in 30 days	Digital Product	User 8892, last login 8/3
High-Risk Vend.	Supplier with risk score ≥80	Risk Score ≥80	Risk	Vendor 302 (labor risk flagged)

Changing the Narrative –The Narrative Reframing Playbook (Canvas for Section 6)

Words shape perception, and perception shapes behavior. When people hear "governance," they often think of compliance, rules, and enforcement. That narrative breeds resistance and fatigue. To succeed, organizations must change the story. They must reframe governance as a catalyst, not a constraint. The Narrative Reframing Playbook is the artifact that makes this possible.

The playbook provides talking points, analogies, and stories that shift the narrative. It presents old narratives alongside new ones. "Governance slows us down" becomes "Governance accelerates decisions by creating trust." "Governance is about control" becomes "Governance is about clarity." These shifts alter how people perceive governance, which in turn influences their response to it.

For executives, the playbook provides messaging that can be used in town halls and board meetings. For managers, it includes language for team discussions. For practitioners, it provides stories they can share peer-to-peer. Over time, these narratives spread faster than any policy document. They embed governance into culture by changing the way people talk about it.

Critics may dismiss narrative as mere words, but words are powerful. They influence emotion, which drives behavior. A single story of governance preventing a failed AI project can do more to build support than a dozen policy documents. The Narrative Reframing Playbook captures these stories and makes them shareable. It turns governance from something people avoid into something they advocate.

The playbook is not static. It evolves as new stories emerge, as culture shifts, and as AI raises new stakes. It ensures that the narrative of governance keeps pace with the reality of data. Without it, old perceptions linger and progress stalls. With it, governance becomes recognized as what it truly is: the catalyst for trust, speed, and value.

Canvas Development and Use

One of the greatest barriers to data governance success isn't technical—it's narrative. Too many programs are introduced as rules, restrictions, and checklists for compliance. That framing drains energy, triggers resistance, and makes governance feel like a burden rather than an accelerator. If you want to light a spark, you must deliberately change the story.

This artifact helps shift conversations from "you must comply" to "you will gain value." It provides practitioners with the tools to collect objections, craft concise reframes, attach credible evidence, and reinforce stories that stick. By reorienting governance as a catalyst—something that enables speed, trust, and innovation—you replace skepticism with belief. Done right, this creates a flywheel where each proof builds more buy-in, and each story makes the next rollout easier.

How to Gather the Inputs

1. **Collect myths and objections from past rollouts.** Every rollout leaves a trail of resistance: "This slows me down," "It's just red tape," or "We already have a process." Gathering these myths systematically creates raw material for the narrative shift. Don't treat objections as complaints—treat them as opportunities to rewrite the story.

2. **Draft value reframes with soundbites tailored to each audience.** Executives, managers, and practitioners care about different things. Executives want outcomes, managers want process clarity, and practitioners want less friction. Craft short reframes that speak directly to each group, avoiding jargon and focusing on benefits they'll feel.

3. **Attach proof: metrics, screenshots, and stories.** A new story without evidence is just marketing. Pair every reframe with data (metrics), visuals (screenshots of improved dashboards),

or anecdotes (short success stories). These proofs anchor the narrative and help people believe change is possible.

4. **Define a clear call-to-action and channel.** Narratives die if they don't drive action. Specify what you want people to do differently, whether it's adopting a glossary, participating in a governance forum, or using a certified dataset. Choose the channel—newsletter, town hall, or Slack—that reliably reaches your audience.

5. **Track message uptake quarterly.** A changed narrative must be reinforced. Survey your audiences, monitor adoption rates, and address any remaining objections. This creates a feedback loop where you can see which messages stick, which fail, and where fresh reframes are needed.

Canvas Field Guide

- **Audience**: Defines who the message is aimed at—Executive, Manager, or Practitioner. Different audiences require different reframes to land effectively.

- **Old Narrative**: The myth, complaint, or pain statement that currently dominates the conversation. Capturing this explicitly ensures you address the real source of resistance rather than guessing.

- **New Value Narrative**: The reframed story that emphasizes benefits. This should flip the objection into an advantage, showing how governance accelerates outcomes rather than obstructs them.

- **Core Soundbite**: A short, memorable line that people can repeat. Good soundbites travel fast—they make your narrative sticky.

- **Proof Point**: A metric, screenshot, or success story that makes the soundbite credible. This is where belief is built.

- **Objection Handling**: A prepared response to pushback. Instead of dismissing objections, meet them head-on with empathy and facts.

- **Call to Action**: The specific step you want your audience to take next. Without a call to action, even the best narrative fizzles.

- **Channel and Cadence**: Where the message will be delivered and how often. Governance narratives fail when they are "one and done." Repetition matters.

- **Spokesperson**: The person who delivers the message. This could be a data leader, but sometimes a peer or respected manager carries more credibility.

- **Status**: Whether the narrative is planned, actively being delivered, or already proven effective. Tracking status keeps the communication portfolio managed and intentional.

Canvas Ignitor

If you want culture to change, the story must change first. This playbook equips you with soundbites, proof points, and reframed narratives that turn governance into an accelerator.

Sample Canvas Layout

- **Columns**: Audience, Old Narrative, New Narrative, Soundbite, Proof Point.

- **Rows**: Each targeted message.

Examples (fields that confuse most):

Audience	Old Narrative	New Narrative	Soundbite	Proof Point
Executive	Governance slows us down	Governance speeds confident decisions	"Trust speeds decisions."	Cycle-time ↓ 22% post-stew.
Manager	This is extra work	Embedded steps reduce rework	"Do it once, use it always."	Rework tickets ↓ 35%.
Practitioner	No one agrees on terms	Glossary aligns definitions	"Same words, same numbers."	Variance disputes ↓ 50%.
Executive	AI is risky	Governed data makes AI scalable	"Governed in, trusted out."	Forecast accuracy ↑ 6 pts.
Manager	People won't adopt	Micro-wins drive adoption	"Small wins, big belief."	78% pilot adoption.

Field Guide Summary

This extra section is designed to be shared, pulled out, and put to work immediately. Each Canvas is a practical way to take the concepts in *Data Catalyst³ (Cubed)* and make them actionable in your organization. The checklists, matrices, maps, glossaries, and playbooks are not overhead. They are catalysts—tools that make it easier for people to align, trust, adopt, and accelerate.

The power of these artifacts lies not in their complexity but in their clarity. Each one makes it harder for excuses to persist and easier for progress to be visible. Use them. Share them. Pin them to the walls of your projects. Because when governance, change, and literacy are combined and operationalized through simple but powerful canvases, that's when the spark becomes a fire.

Index

www.ingramcontent.com/pod-product-compliance
Lightning Source LLC
Chambersburg PA
CBHW060931220326
41597CB00020BA/3483